Nita,

Keep

dreaming! ♡

Ready to be Heard

How I Lost My Hearing and Found My Voice

Amanda McDonough

BALBOA.
PRESS

A DIVISION OF HAY HOUSE

Balboa Press books may be ordered through booksellers or by contacting:

Balboa Press
A Division of Hay House
1663 Liberty Drive
Bloomington, IN 47403
www.balboapress.com
1 (877) 407-4847

Print information available on the last page.

ISBN: 978-1-9822-0109-8 (sc)
ISBN: 978-1-9822-0111-1 (hc)
ISBN: 978-1-9822-0110-4 (e)

Library of Congress Control Number: 2018903806

Balboa Press rev. date: 04/27/2018

To the dreamers, the doers, and the helpers who ignore human limits and social norms to do everything they can to make this world a better place—especially my mother, who loves and gives without ever expecting anything in return. You are my hero.

CONTENTS

Acknowledgments

I would like to thank my family for all of their support while I wrote this book and for putting up with me working on vacations, holidays, and birthdays.

Thank you to the Frishman brothers for encouraging me to put my story to paper and for checking in on my progress as wrote it down.

Big thanks to Aarika Allura; Andzej Malins; Grandmother; my mother; and my brother, Andrew, for being my guinea pigs and reading the first several awful drafts of this book—which have since been destroyed to save everyone else from ever having to experience them.

Thanks to Kevlyn Walsh for creating my first mock cover of this book and Face' for letting me use the great headshot he took of me for that mock cover.

Big thanks to the awesome Starley Murray for teaching me how to do television interviews so that I don't look as awkward when addressing the public as I feel in real life.

Special thanks to my uncles, Roy, Doug, Mark, Jim, and Tim; my aunts, Rene, Jayia, PJ, and Chrissy; my cousins, Paula, Anthony, Katie, Delainey, Stephanie, Gino, Ryan, Mitch, Kim, Nichole, Jonny, Joey, and Valeria; and all of my amazing family in Boston and Las Vegas, as well as abroad in Europe. I love you all dearly! Thanks for all the memories that helped me fill these pages!

Thank you to my grandmother for always telling it like it is and barging into the room singing random songs to make me smile whenever I felt overwhelmed while writing this book.

Thanks to Mishael and Ann at So, You Want to Write! for helping me edit and get the final version of this book together. You guys helped me get over that final hump, and I am so grateful.

Big thanks to Natasha Jimenez for the book cover photo shoot.

I want to express my gratitude for everyone I wrote about within these pages. You all helped me become the person I am today, and I will always be grateful for that.

To my friends, thanks for putting up with me disappearing for weeks at a time into my work, for still loving me despite my terrible texting skills, and for accepting my quirky personality.

Thank you to the Deaf community and my Deaf friends for teaching me so much and helping me to grow in my identity.

Thanks to the creator, producers, writers, cast, and crew of *Switched at Birth* for creating something that had such a positive impact on my life.

To the Walt Disney Company, thank you for providing me with such wonderful employment experiences in my youth.

Big thanks to God for guiding me through all these trials in my life and helping me to become a better, stronger, more faithful person.

Lastly, but definitely not least, I would like to thank my mom for encouraging me to keep going on days that this book felt like it would never be finished. ˆ

INTRODUCTION

I wrote this book because I was crazy enough to want to change the world. I wanted to make life better for those going through a loss—whether it is a loss of a sense, mobility, identity, a loved one, or a friend. I wanted to show those who are struggling that anything is possible if you never give up on yourself. I wanted to encourage others to change their perspective, become the hero of their own story, and tell their story to the world.

Every human on this planet has his or her own personal struggles. Mine is no worse or better than yours. How we chose to respond to our struggles is what sets us apart.

No human is perfect, and I am no exception. I have made my fair share of mistakes, responded to situations in ways I regretted later, learned from some of my wrongs, and repeated many others before life's lessons finally got through to me.

This is the story of how I gradually lost my hearing. This is the tale of how life taught me to overcome my fears and reclaim my voice in a way that many would consider cruel.

When I lost the last of my hearing, a piece of me died. In the darkness of that pain, I chose to find hope. I discovered a new culture and language, and, most importantly, I uncovered who I truly am. Sometimes it takes defeat to reveal what really matters in life.

Today I am happy. I live an amazing life. I wrote *Ready to Be Heard* in the hopes that it would help others find their happiness. I wrote it in hope that it would help others realize that they are not alone and in the hope that it would inspire some to learn something new, meet someone new, try something new, empathize with someone new, or simply think something new.

Writing these pages was also therapeutic. Every word is my own. There is no ghostwriter, no fancy editor who rearranged my story. Putting these words to paper helped me realize how far I really have come in my life and how much I have grown.

It all started when I decided that my voice mattered, that my story had power, and that I could achieve my dreams and help others achieve theirs. I hope that, by the time you finish reading these pages, you will find the strength behind your own story to tackle your struggles and assist others in tackling theirs, because everyone has a story, and no one should have to struggle alone. You can make a difference. Together we can change the world for the better. This book started when I decided that I was ready to be heard.

Part 1

CHOOSING TO HAVE NO LIMITS

I don't use the word "can't" because I don't believe in limiting myself. I am able. I am capable. I am strong. Never think less of yourself because society expects you to behave a certain way. We decide our own limits. I have chosen to have none.

—Amanda McDonough

1

ONCE UPON A TIME:
THE FIRST FOUR YEARS

Birth

"Once upon a time, there was a wonderful little girl who lived on the top of a hill." My grandmother started every story she ever told about me this way, so it is only fitting that I begin my story the same way. You see, I look at life as a story. I see the world in the frames of a movie, and every different chapter of my life feels like a new act in a play.

So who is this wonderful little girl who grew up on a hill? Well, she was born a princess, like all other little girls.

On a magical night in March 1990, my mother went into labor with her first child. My father rushed my mother to the hospital, just to learn that it could take hours before she was really ready to have the baby. So, naturally, they walked across the street to a movie theater and watched the newest Sean Connery and James Earl Jones film, *The Hunt for Red October*, before returning to the hospital to give birth to me.

I was born with a full head of jet-black, tightly curly hair and the deepest black eyes my parents had ever seen. My skin was porcelain—so white it almost glowed. My father looked at my round, chubby face and tiny body; turned to my mother; and, with an amused look on his face, inquired, "Did you cheat on me with an Eskimo?"

They named me Amanda. The name was picked from a 1990's

baby-name book. My mother and father, Julie and Joe, had the most common names of their generation, and my father wanted to give me a name that would stand out from the crowd. Gertrude is the name he picked, but my mother had Amanda written on my birth certificate before my father could sweeten the deal with the possibility of the nickname Gertie. My name means "loved by all," which definitely set the tone for the type of life I would lead.

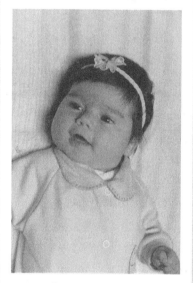

Amanda McDonough as a baby.

Big Crazy Italian Irish American Family

My parents are the definition of "opposites attract." My father is a logical introvert who prefers to spend his time alone. He was raised in a military family and developed a very strong demeanor. His mother often jokes that he was born a man. As a child, he saved and invested his allowance instead of spending it on temporary pleasures like candy like his three brothers did. My father emphasized education, respect, and proper oral hygiene when we were children.

He prided himself on the fact that he had never changed a diaper in his life. I am not joking. There is actually a story about him being left with me, for the first (and only) time, as an infant. Apparently at some point I pooped my diaper, as all infants do, and my father's reaction was to put me in my car seat and drive me fifteen minutes to his parents' house in West Covina so that he could trick his mother into changing my diaper and act like he didn't know it was dirty to begin with. From him, I inherited my frugalness, practicality, ability to spend time alone, eyes, and this funny little freckle on my ear that is in the exact same place as his.

I get most of my personality traits from my mother, who is a bubbly, friendly, talkative extrovert. My mother makes friends everywhere she goes. She is always volunteering for different committees or events and is superinvolved in the community. She always thinks of others before herself; oftentimes, I have to remind her to take care of herself too. This probably comes from being the second oldest of six kids and always being the one to help care for the younger siblings. She was born in Boston, Massachusetts; moved to California when she was young; and adopted a Californian accent like her peers. My brother and I always knew we were in serious trouble when Mom would suddenly drop her r's and her Bostonian accent would emerge—"paahk the cahh in the Havaahd Yahhd" status.

Being a biological mixture of these polar opposite people has basically made me a walking contradiction, whose personality and preferences make it impossible for me to fit into any existing stereotype.

Amanda's mom and dad,
Julie and Joe, as newlyweds.

During my childhood, my mother owned and operated a successful real estate and loans company called AmeriSell Advantage Properties. My father worked for Hewlett Packard. His job required him to travel often and kept him away from home. My mom's job required her to work long hours. However, I was never deprived of attention or love as a child because I had a huge extended family eager and ready to pitch in. People say, "It takes a village to raise a child." Well, I felt like I had my own small country helping to raise me.

The members of my mom's family remind me of characters from *My Big Fat Greek Wedding.* Only we aren't Greek. We are Italian. Biologically, I am technically more Irish than Italian, but the Italian American heritage is strong with me, just like the force. Pastas, pizzas, breadsticks, carbs, and more carbs are what my family was raised on. My grandmother's blood is probably half tomato sauce and garlic at this point.

That woman can cook. She was so used to cooking to feed her six children, herself, her husband (my Papas), her nieces, her nephews, and whatever guests came over that she never quite figured out how to cook in smaller quantities. It's like she is cooking for an entire village every time she makes anything.

I was the firstborn child of my generation on my mother's side. That made me the first baby for her five siblings to spoil, and spoil me they did. I have so many fond memories of my childhood. These include learning to climb the olive tree outside my great-grandmother Nana's retirement community as she carefully looked on with her Italian dark-cocoa skin and red Lucille Ball hair.

I have fond memories of dancing to Frank Sinatra with my grandmother in her kitchen as we sang into wooden spoons. We would spin around in our cooking aprons as we held the notes along with Old Blue Eyes. And I have memories of treasure hunts with my Papas, my mother's father, and being lowered into barrels filled with freshly raked leaves just to throw them up in the air while exclaiming with joy so that he would have to start all over.

I have memories of playing in my father's parents' garden, hiding within the rows of shrubbery and waiting for someone to discover me. And I have memories of my first time drinking out of a soda bottle on my own, thanks to the dedicated and patient training of my aunt PJ.

I had a blessed childhood that many would envy.

Until, that is, one fateful night in January 1994, when my monopoly on my parents' attention and reign over the hearts of all of my extended family members ended. Andrew Quinton McDonough was born. My father was excited to have a son. It helped that my brother looked like a clone of my father from day one.

I had to admit he was pretty cute, and I decided to take my big-sister duties seriously. I was really protective of that tiny kid from the first day my mom sat me on our couch, put a pillow in my lap, and gently lowered this tiny bundle of a boy into my arms while repeating, "Support the head, support the head, support the head," at varying levels of distress.

A few months after my brother was born, my mom's brother, Roy, had a daughter. Then her sister, Jayia, had a daughter two days later. The family was growing. I was no longer the center of everyone's attention.

*Some of Amanda's family members from both
the Amicangioli and McDonough sides.*

Born Performer

From the moment I was born, it was obvious that I loved to perform. I was constantly dancing around and singing for anyone who would listen, whether my listeners were family members, friends, or complete strangers on the street. Stranger danger was not a lesson that resonated well with me as a child; I wanted to make everyone smile.

When I was two years old, I took a ballet class. I loved leaping around the hardwood floors and watching my pink leotard-wearing reflection in the large mirrored walls. Unfortunately, I was also a klutz. While the other girls would do a plié, I wobbled. As they leaped, I stumbled. And on more than one occasion, I took a few other innocent ballerinas down with me as I full-on fell. Their parents looked on through the observation window in horror as I knocked the other tutu-clad ballerinas down like dominos in my attempt to bow gracefully.

That was the last straw. The dance moms got together and decided that, for the well-being of all involved, I should "try a less balance-oriented form of dance." They actually kicked a two-year-old out of beginner's ballet!

Still, two-year-old little Amanda didn't give up on the art of dance. It would eventually take me failing to master beginner's classes in jazz, tap, line dancing, and hip-hop before I finally accepted that dancing just wasn't my thing. That is a realization that, to this day, I tend to be violently reminded of whenever I try out the latest dance trend. Like the dab. I can't dab. It just isn't physically possible.

Amanda's first tap recital.

However, I did discover my thing two short years after my dreams of being a prima ballerina flopped. One day, when I was watching television with my mother, I had an epiphany. I realized that the people on the show were real and were doing real things, but they were just pretending. I asked my mother for a word to explain this phenomenon. She gave me the word—*acting*.

I was instantly obsessed. I knew in that very moment in the very fiber of my being, in every hair in my ribbon-wrapped pigtails, in every fleck of brown in my big brown eyes, that I wanted to be an actress. No, I *needed* to be an actress. This was my destiny. So, I exclaimed with as much conviction as my tiny voice could muster, "I am going to be an actress!"

My mother looked at me and simply said, "Okay."

2

CAN YOU HEAR ME NOW?
THE DIAGNOSIS

Preschool

When I was about two and a half years old (the half part is important to children, so I made sure to add that in there to appease my inner child), I started at FunShine Preschool. FunShine was a great school managed by none other than my aunt and godmother, Jayia. This is probably the only reason I got in without having a full handle on the whole potty training thing.

For nearly two years, I was the reigning queen of the preschool playground. Like a tornado, my big personality and endless energy could not be stopped by any human. I surrounded myself with friends and decided I was the leader. Every day, I would choose what game was to be played.

To put it lightly, I was bossy. I hated nap time, and I was so stubborn that I refused to stay in my cot. So the teachers would have me help them prepare snacks for the other students while everyone else slept. I loved the special treatment! I lived for standing out and being recognized.

I was a smart, confident kid, and the routine of going to school each day worked well for me. We learned things like our colors, numbers, and letters and how to share. We made macaroni art, finger painted, and played pretend. I had a head start on reading and insisted on helping my mom and dad read my bedtime stories each night.

At one point, in an attempt to impress my dad, I insisted on reading him Dr. Seuss' *Green Eggs and Ham* on my own one night. At first, he was amazed, as I got every single word right—until he realized I was turning the pages at the wrong times.

It turned out I had memorized the entire book and was reciting it to him accurately from memory and just acting like I was reading it. As the nights passed and more books were added to my repertoire, I started to grow up. In the blink of an eye, I went from being a toddler to a big girl.

FunShine offered vision and hearing tests to all their students. When I was four years old, my parents signed a permission slip, allowing me to participate in these tests of my senses. I was great at tests, and I loved the praise I got for doing things well. So, as instructed, I lined up, correcting a few of the other students who were not forming a straight line and waited as patiently as a four-year-old can for her turn.

I don't remember taking the test. I don't remember the nurse who administered it. I don't remember the room I was in when it happened. What I do remember was the look of worry in my aunt's eyes when my mother picked me up that day. I remember the look of disbelief and almost distain as my mother listened to what my aunt had to say. Something had happened. I could feel it. It was something bad. Yet I had no idea what it was.

Diagnosis

Shortly thereafter, my mother took me to the doctor. I was afraid they would give me a shot, because doctors are nothing more than evil shot administers to four-year-olds. They may hide behind a smile and a lollipop and think they have us fooled, but every four-year-old knows that this is only a facade.

This was a new doctor. He took a cone-shaped little hammer and looked in my ears, my nose, and my throat. He put weird headphones in my ears that built up pressure and had me look at an electronic race car.

I repeated the words "airplane, race car, ice cream, hotdog, and beach ball" over and over again.

Then he put me in a small black padded room with a thick, heavy metal door. There was one giant window but the rest of the room was covered in a padding. A clear glass box hung on one wall with a monkey holding symbols in it. A second one held a stuffed bear. He pressed a button to make the monkey move in an attempt to lighten the mood.

They sat me on an old wooden child's chair, and he asked me to react to each of the sounds as I heard them in the room like a game. My mother was with me, and she watched eagerly. I knew this was a test. I didn't understand why I was being tested, but a few minutes into the "game," a look of sadness came over my mother's face, and I knew I wasn't winning.

"Mild hearing loss" was the term the doctor used as he placed a white photocopied graph in front of my mother with X's and O's connected by lines drawn on it. The doctor couldn't tell her what had caused the hearing loss. It could have been anything from an illness to exposure to loud sounds, medication, head trauma, or nerve damage. The list went on.

He couldn't tell her if this was a one-time drop in hearing or if it would get worse for me with time. My mother asked a few questions and then turned to look at me, a four-year-old whose patience had run out and who was fidgeting in the seat next to her.

How would she explain this to her precious little girl? How does anyone sit down a child and explain to her that she has lost something, something precious, something that everyone else around her has and that she can never get back? I can't imagine this was easy.

When my father came home that night, my mother filled him in, and then they told me together.

At first, I didn't understand. Their entire world had changed. The way they looked at me, the way they treated me during that conversation had changed. Yet I didn't feel any different. I didn't really notice the "hearing loss." What I did notice, however, was how differently people looked at me now that I had it.

The Promise

I decided at four years old that, since I didn't feel any different, I didn't want anyone to treat me any differently. So, being a stubborn, bossy little girl, I swore my parents to secrecy. I figured that, if no one knew I was different, then no one would treat me differently. Therefore, I wouldn't be different. Problem solved.

Technically, I was just in denial and avoiding dealing with my problems, but at four years old, it seemed like the logical thing to do. I went about my life as normal, playing, reading, performing, and learning like any other kid my age. I let this hearing loss diagnosis fall into the back of my mind and be nearly forgotten.

Parents in Denial

My parents had a harder time forgetting about my diagnosis than I did. Here they were with a doctor telling them that their child was losing her hearing. Yet the doctors couldn't tell them what to expect, what to plan for, or what to do. To them, they had a happy, smart, social child who didn't even seem to notice she had lost any hearing.

It didn't seem to affect me at all. The doctors reassured my parents that this may have just been a one-time loss and told them to bring me back in every six months to monitor for any changes. They offered my parents no resources or information that could help them learn how this could affect me in the future or how to navigate raising a child with hearing loss.

Since I didn't appear to be in pain or struggling due to this new medical development, they decided to just let me continue to be the happy little girl they knew and not to scare me or complicate my life by trying to force on me any additional help that I didn't appear to need. I think a part of them was in denial too, that anything like this could be happening to their perfect little girl. It was easier for all of us to just try to ignore it and go back to our normal lives.

3

PLAYING THE PART:
GRADUAL DECLINE IN HEARING

Trying to Fit in

I started kindergarten with the same confidence that I'd had when I'd ruled over the playground at my aunt's preschool. I walked straight up to my peers, held out my little hand, and said, "Hi, I'm Amanda. Let's be friends." That was that. By the end of my first day of kindergarten, I already had a great group of friends surrounding me. We dug for worms, played dress up, finger painted, and chased each other around the playground.

Chelsea, Juliette, Megan, Emily, Brianna, Savannah, and I grew superclose. We joined Girl Scouts together. We took up AYSO soccer (which, four years later, I finally added to the same list as dance—it wasn't my thing). Our crew had constant playdates at each other's homes, pool parties, and outings. Even our moms became best friends! There is really no better feeling when you are a kid than knowing you have friends—real, consistent, fun friends.

As we got older, I started to actually notice myself not being able to hear things as well, and that scared me. I was afraid my pretty and popular friend group wouldn't accept me if they knew I was different—that I was not quite whole somehow. I began acting like I could hear everything that they did.

Before I knew it, I wasn't just acting like I could hear. I was acting like a completely different person. I was pretending to like all the same things they did and saying things I didn't actually believe in. I was acting like the person I thought my friends wanted me to be. I felt like I was living a double life. On the outside, everyone saw a pretty, social young girl who did well in school, was involved in lots of after-school activities, and appeared happy. Inside, I was conflicted.

I grew up in a one-story house on the top of a hill overlooking a valley through which the 60 Freeway flowed (if you can say any California freeway "flows"). The house was at the very end of the street on a cul-de-sac, and it was a great place for kids to play. There was no street traffic because it was a dead end, and no unwanted strangers came up there because the hill was so steep.

On that street, there were four other kids who my brother and I played with. They were brother and sister teams too. We ended up joining forces and forming a pretty respectable child gang up on that hill. With them, I could forget about my problems and just play.

We played soccer and basketball, rode bikes, and hung out in each others' backyards. It was a pretty cool way to grow up. We were outside many nights until the streetlights came on. But from the time that first bell rang at school until the time the last bell rang, we didn't know each other. It was kind of like, "The first rule about fight club is: you do not talk about fight club"—kind of unspoken agreement.

On that cul-de-sac, I was safe. I could be myself. But back in that school yard, I was becoming more and more self-conscious. I couldn't stop myself from seeing everyone else around me as better than me.

Doctors' Appointments and Hearing Tests

When you are a child growing up with hearing loss, you spend a lot of time with ENTs, audiologists, and specialists. They test your hearing at least two times a year and run blood work, CT scans, MRIs, and anything they can think of to see if they can "fix" you and save your hearing. I saw them all, every specialist, every audiologist, every clinic. My parents made sure I got the best care possible.

I grew up in these cold little five-foot-by-five-foot soundproof padded rooms, with one thick metal door and one clear glass window that allowed the doctors to observe me like a zoo animal. Mechanical monkeys, cymbals in hand, hung on the walls in clear boxes in an attempt to cheer up the room's sad young occupants.

They would lock me alone in there to take my hearing tests with a small black button in hand and heavy headphones crushing my tiny ears, afraid of failing, afraid of being alone, but mostly afraid of the silence.

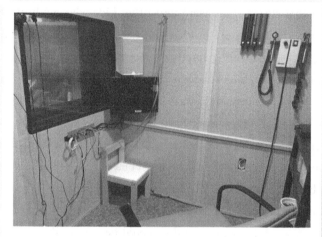

A soundproof hearing test booth.

They were all the same—the rooms, the doctors, the tests. Year in and year out, I would find myself trapped. The doctor would run tests and then hand my parents a piece of paper, one that had obviously been photocopied too many times, with two graphs on it. One graph would be labeled left and one labeled right—one for each of my ears. They tracked the progress of my hearing loss.

The top of the graph represented "normal hearing," the bottom, complete silence. Over the years, I watched as the little X's and O's descended down the chart, closer and closer to the bottom. I watched as my mother tried not to cry each time the doctor handed her that innocent-looking piece of paper, and she compared my steady decline to the previous one. Every time, I left those offices feeling like a failure.

My parents took me everywhere to try to find answers, from Primary Care Physicians to hearing clinics to Whittier Hearing Center to the Los Angeles Children's Hospital (LACH). Everywhere I went, it was the same tests, the same rooms, and the same graphs.

No one could tell my parents why I was losing my hearing. "Nerve damage," they kept saying. There was no cause offered and no cure. They couldn't even tell my mother if I would continue to lose my hearing or if it would stabilize. All we could do was hope for the best as we walked out of those appointments.

The audiograms were showing that my right ear was declining more rapidly than my left, which was doing its best to stay stable. The way hearing loss happens is strange. It isn't like turning down the radio, where all sounds decrease at the same rate at the same time. With hearing loss, you lose certain frequencies before others.

I was losing my high-pitched frequencies. The sound of birds, flutes, and the beeping of our microwave at home began to dim. I struggled to hear them until they became nothing more than a memory. I looked at the birds that built their nests every year in the rafters of our home.

I watched them fly around, their brown wings stretched towards the sky. I watched as the baby birds hatched and opened their beaks wide, like I did every year, calling for their mother. This year, I strained to hear their cries. Yet no matter how hard I tried, before I even reached my sixth birthday, their calls to their mother were lost to my young ears.

I learned pretty early in life that, even though the doctors were great at assigning the little X's and O's that represented my hearing on a chart, they didn't seem to actually understand what my life with hearing loss was like. They could tell me what I should and shouldn't be able to hear. But in reality, I had good days, and I had bad days.

Some days, I literally could forget I had any hearing loss at all. I understood everything going on around me seamlessly. Those days, I felt like I could do anything. Confidence and happiness pulsed through my veins. It was euphoric not needing to constantly worry about sound. I could actually just focus on being a kid, on being me. Other days, the bad days, I struggled with the most basic of tasks.

Communicating and focusing in school felt impossible. On these days, I was constantly straining—not just my ears, but also my eyes and my entire body, trying to understand anything happening around me. On these days, I became shy, frustrated, and tense and kept to myself as much as I could.

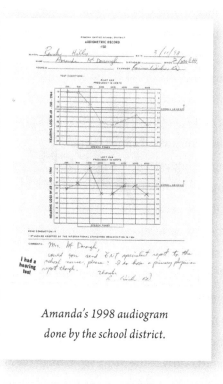

Amanda's 1998 audiogram
done by the school district.

It upset me that these X's and O's on a piece of paper told me I should be able to hear certain things, but in loud or distracting environments, I couldn't.

It was one thing to hear a beep and press a button in a quiet controlled room designed specifically for hearing tests and another thing completely to actually hear the end-of-lunch bell in a cafeteria filled with rowdy elementary school kids or to understand when a friend invited me to go on the slide during a seven-year-old's chaotic Chuck E. Cheese birthday party.

The doctors may have studied hearing loss in school, but it became apparent the more often I saw them that they didn't actually understand what I was going through. I resented them a little for this. They were supposed to have answers for me. They were supposed to help me—to fix me even.

Yet they didn't actually understand the shame and embarrassment I was going through every day when I misheard a sentence or missed information all together. They didn't understand the culture and psyche of a person going through hearing loss, let alone a child going through it. Because they didn't understand any of this, I was forced to figure it out on my own as I went along.

I needed support, not just medically, but also psychologically and socially. My doctors only looked at my decreasing hearing as a physical problem. All they could do was "monitor" my hearing as it continued to decrease. They couldn't stop it, tell me why it was happening, identify any triggers, or even give me the resources I needed to get through it on an everyday basis, which made them useless to an elementary school kid.

I continued to do my best with what I had, because that is literally all I could do. I had no other choices. My parents did what they could to try to help me through it all. But at the end of the day, on that playground, in that classroom, at that one kid's birthday party, this was my cross to bear, not theirs. I was the one who had to live with this struggle every second of every day.

My mom held onto this hope that my hearing would stabilize and that I would be fine. They just wanted what was best for their little girl but didn't know what that was and weren't given the resources to find out.

You have to remember this was the '90s, before the Internet was superpopular and connected millions of people with the click of a button, allowing them to share information on their personal lives and experiences freely with others. Medical journals, magazines, a local library, my doctors, and their immediate circle of friends were the only sources of information on hearing loss that they had access to.

Just like my mom, I too held onto that tiny little piece of hope that my hearing would stabilize. I actually convinced myself it was the truth because the alternative was too scary and I refused to even let myself think about it. The word *deaf* wasn't even one used around me by my doctors or parents. It was a distant, unknown concept that I kept myself oblivious to. *Hearing impaired* were the words they sometimes used—two words that, together, left a bad taste in my mouth and that I chose to ignore.

So, the good hearing days and bad hearing days continued to dictate my mood and my level of functioning as I clung to a couple sentences uttered by one of my many doctors near the beginning of my hearing-loss journey. "It is possible that her hearing will stabilize. She won't be able to regain any of the lost hearing, but it is possible that this is as bad as it is going to get."

I can't even remember the name or face of the doctor who said it, but I held onto these two sentences, like a hiker dangling off the edge of a cliff overlooking the Grand Canyon, for dear life.

The most frustrating thing about this experience was that no matter how many doctors we visited, no matter how many tests I took, and no matter how hard I prayed, no one could ever give me any of the answers I was seeking. Why was this happening to me? What was causing it? Would my hearing stabilize? Would I lose it forever? Is there anything I can do to stop my hearing from declining?

Hearing Aids

By the time I was seven, my hearing had decreased to the point where it was suggested that I would benefit from these devices called hearing aids. Basically, they were small machines that fit over my ears and had molds created to fit to my uniquely small ear canal.

They had an on/off switch, a dial to turn the volume up or down, and a hatch at the bottom to put in fresh batteries. I was fitted with my first pair of bilateral hearing aids, one hearing aid in each ear, at Whittier Hearing Center. My parents bought them for me.

They cost them roughly five thousand dollars out of pocket; insurance companies saw hearing aids as a vanity item, not a necessity. This posture is ridiculous—to this day I have never met anyone who wore hearing aids for fun instead of simply to function.

I don't really remember putting them on for the first time. I have a vague memory of my first hearing aid fitting experience; the doctor squirted a cold, slimy, almost Play-Doh like substance into each of my ears, and I waited with my head tilted to one side for the mush to harden and form a hard waxy mold of the inside of my ear.

What I do have a strong memory of is how they made me feel. They felt weird. My ears felt plugged from the soft plastic pieces inside of them. They would itch and make my inner ear sweat. Hearing through them felt wrong. The sound wasn't normal or natural. It all felt computerized.

There was this strange hum in every sound that I had never experienced before but kind of reminded me of the sound distortion of old amps from the '60s. It was a slightly computerized, almost echoey rounded-out sound that was laid over every frequency I heard. I had to remind myself that this was supposed to be a good thing, but it felt like a punishment.

I do remember my second fitting for new hearing aids, several years later when I was in seventh grade. Digital hearing aids had just become available. I can only assume that my first experience was similar.

My mom, the specialist, and I were inside a booth similar to the little soundproof hearing test rooms with a thick heavy metal door, cold gray walls, and one big window.

The difference was that inside this room was a desk, a computer with fancy equipment attached to it, and two chairs for visitors. The hearing aid specialist used my most recent hearing test to make adjustments to the hearing aids through his computer. A long wire ran from an external drive attached to the computer. It was pinned to my shirt and ran up into the hearing aids on my ears.

He adjusted a series of levers on his computer screen, increasing the volume of certain frequencies that my tests showed my ears struggled with. He asked questions like, "Is that comfortable?" "Is it too loud, too soft, or just right?" I answered the questions to the best of my ability.

I was a kid with hearing loss. I didn't know what "just right" meant anymore. At this point in my life, some sounds were becoming a distant memory for me. Eventually, he finished, unhooked the wires from my hearing aids and the front of my shirt, and asked me to test them out outside of the little soundproof booth, which happened to be inside a Costco, a popular warehouse bulk grocery store chain.

I took one step inside the store, and immediately I was overwhelmed by sounds. There were sounds of people talking far away from me, of shopping carts rolling on linoleum, of items being moved, of feet hitting the floor as people walked along the aisles, and of boxes being picked up and put down as shoppers examined the packages. The sounds flooded my brain. It was too much information. It was too much sound. It was too loud. But most of all, it was wrong. All of the sounds flowed through the hearing aids into my ear canal and finally reaching my brain, sounding like they were being processed through the same old mics and amps as the Beatles songs I loved to listen to with my uncle and cousins. I took off the hearing aids. I was angry. I felt gypped. They had told me these machines would help me, but instead they frustrated me.

Every time I went in for an adjustment, I experienced conflicting emotions. Sometimes I would hear sounds I hadn't heard in a long time and feel really happy and lucky to have my hearing aids. Other times I would get my hopes up that an adjustment to my hearing aids might make a certain sound easier for me to hear and end up disappointed. Sometimes I would get angry that I even needed these things on my ears.

One thing remained the same, though. I hid behind my mother every time we came out of that hearing aid booth, hoping that no one we knew happened to be shopping that day and would spot me, revealing my secret.

Amanda's hearing aids over the years.

When I was seven and had just received my first pair of hearing aids, my parents had to force me to wear them to school for the first time. I wore my hair down to hide the unwanted machines that now took up residence on my tiny ears. They felt heavy in more than one way.

Now, instead of being carefree and playing kick ball or red rover on the playground, I had to be careful of my hearing aids. Now when people hugged me, the hearing aids would let out a loud painful squelch that I came to know as "feedback." For the first time in my life, I walked onto that playground at recess and sat alone on the grass. I was still guarding my secret. No one knew I had hearing loss, and I was determined to keep it that way. I couldn't join my friends; they might hug me. I couldn't join my classmates; they might suggest a physical sport.

I just sat there, alone in the grass making flower crowns and trying to figure out how to adapt to this new change in my life. You see, up until this point, hearing loss had been normal to me. It was all I knew. Every time my hearing declined, I simply adapted and moved forward, but this time was different.

This time, I couldn't act normal because now there were two machines in my ears, two physical constant reminders that I was different. They were reminders that everyone else on that playground had something I didn't have, reinforcing the distorted belief I held that I was lesser than my peers. They could all hear; I couldn't. Therefore, they must be better than me, I reasoned. I became angry with myself, angry with my body, and angry with my ears.

Losing Sounds

As I grew up, my hearing continued to progressively decline, with no obvious triggers. It happened so gradually at first that I hardly noticed. It was little things that started to feel different. I realized everyone in the room was reacting to something that I hadn't heard, a missed word here, or a soft sound where a loud one should be there—little moments that began to add up.

In fourth grade, I decided to learn how to play the violin. It seemed like an elegant and romantic instrument. My parents supported this new way of expressing myself and rented me an old violin from a local music store to learn on. I was a quick study. I loved the feeling of the bow in my delicate hands.

I loved the feeling of the vibrations passing through the body of the violin, touching my chin. Most of all, I loved the sound. To me, there was no sweeter or more pure sound than the ones that came out of the violin. The instrument itself simply bled a romantic, melodic, sweet lullaby that had me mesmerized. I was so proud when I mastered my first song on that violin, "Twinkle, Twinkle, Little Star."

It may not seem like much, but every day, I would rush home and practice. My parents saw how dedicated I had become, and after I had been playing for nearly two years on a hand-me-down rental instrument, they decided to surprise me with my very own brand-new violin that coming Christmas.

I could not have been more excited when I saw that black violin box beneath the Christmas tree with a big red bow on it. I took it out and played my parents a tune. It felt so different in my hands, and the sound that resonated from it was cleaner and crisper than that of the secondhand violin I had become accustomed to. I loved it, and it was mine!

One morning during winter break, I woke up and something felt different. I got out of bed and opened up the slick black violin case with the red bow still proudly wrapped around it. I lifted the freshly finished wood up to my shoulder and placed my chin on it.

I can still remember the smell of the smooth new wood beneath my nose. My bow came to rest on the strings, and I gently slid it across the instrument, playing a C. Nothing happened. I applied more pressure to the bow and tried again. Again, nothing happened. For a moment, I panicked. The thought, *I broke it! Dad is going to kill me!* flashed through my mind. Then, a second later, an even more terrifying thought hit me.

I turned up my hearing aids, changed the note, applied more pressure and tried one last time. I could feel it. The vibrations danced through the wood under my chin. But I heard nothing. In one heartbreaking moment my favorite sound in the world was gone forever, and with it, a little piece of me was lost.

I couldn't tell my parents. They would just take me back to the doctors—doctors who couldn't do anything for me except lock me back in that padded soundproof room for a half an hour and make me acknowledge beeps with a button. No one could help me, no one could save me, and no one could ever bring back the sounds of the violin.

I felt betrayed by my own body. A piece of me was slowly dying, and I couldn't stop it. So, I put the beautifully crafted child's violin in its black case. I put the case on the top shelf of my closet, and I promised myself I would never look at it again.

My parents, the most frugal people on the planet, had spent good money on that violin. Naturally, they nagged me about playing it. Each time I refused and would give them attitude and claim, "I hate the violin," or "The music is stupid." We would argue about it a lot, and they would sometimes be able to force me to screech out a few notes. But eventually, they reluctantly gave up and stopped forcing me to play.

I knew they were confused and disappointed in me, but I figure that was better than them being sad that I was losing something I treasured—my hearing.

The violin was the first sound I truly mourned. It was also the first time I lied to my parents about my hearing loss, but it was definitely not the last. From this point on I made the decision to carry this burden alone. They would never understand what it was like to cling to the memory of sound or to have that memory follow you like a ghost.

I remember watching my classmates perform during the fall concert, my eyes glued on the string section, watching as the bows glided up and down my favorite instrument, remembering what should be there but no longer was. I also remember not letting anyone see me cry after.

I knew my hearing loss caused my parents pain. Each time my mother was handed my latest audiogram, I could see her heart sink. I knew she blamed herself. Somehow she felt my inability to hear was her fault. I refused to let her feel that way anymore. Because of that, hearing loss became my own personal struggle, and I no longer told my parents when my hearing changed.

*Amanda with her violin after performing in
her elementary school orchestra concert.*

Change in My Personality

I had learned over the years that I couldn't control my hearing. I couldn't control how well I did or didn't do on hearing tests. No matter how hard I worked and no matter how badly I wanted to pass, I always failed. Failure began to become a feeling I loathed more than anything.

That is probably why I worked so hard in school. If you pay attention, study, and do the work, then you will ace the class. In class, I had control over how well I did. I was always a straight A student. I read at a level several grades higher than my peers. I even was accepted into the gifted children program, and a new reading program was developed by the school to accommodate me and a few of my peers whose reading levels were quickly exceeding the level of the materials provided in our elementary school library. My parents were so proud of my academic success. The praise I was receiving from them caused me to throw even more of my attention into my studies.

Every night before I went to bed, I began praying. I prayed to God to let me keep what was left of my hearing. I didn't ask for any hearing back—I thought that was greedy—but I just wanted to keep what I had. Every night, I echoed the same plea from my twin bed covered to the brim with stuffed animals.

I offered my stuffed animals as a bargaining chip, offered to be the perfect daughter, or promised straight A's on my spelling tests, but nothing worked. Some days I woke up, and I knew immediately that a sound was lost forever. Other days, I would have no change in my hearing. And on certain days, I would make it halfway through the day before realizing I could no longer extricate a friend's voice or the sound of markers on a whiteboard from the noises around me in the atmosphere.

I somehow got it into my head that, if I was exceptionally well behaved and did really well in school, somehow I would be able to keep my hearing. But that was just another delusion I clung to as I tried to maintain some sense of normalcy in my young life.

Other than my behavior, succeeding academically was the only other thing in my life that I had control over. Doing well in school wasn't easy for me, though. I had to ask to sit in the front of the classroom. I started positioning myself at the lunch table so that everyone was on my left side, aka my good hearing side. I made sure to always walk on everyone's right so that my good ear could listen to the conversation, and I noticed myself focusing more on people's lips as they talked.

I had to study twice as hard as everyone else to keep up in class, but no one seemed to notice the extra effort. I got labeled as one of the "smart girls," and I was proud of that label. I worked hard for that label.

Despite the fact that I had become a bit of a nerd, the rest of my group of friends had become the elementary equivalent of a "mean girls" group. They wore clothes from Banana Republic, styled their hair in the latest trends, and found joy in gossiping about other little girls.

I had become a bit chubby. I wore the same Adidas blue and purple jacket nearly every day. And as my insecurities with my hearing grew, they started to take notice. They were like sharks drawn to blood, and I was bleeding. I knew I would eventually make it on their list of people to destroy, so I tried to just blend in and go with the flow whenever I was around them.

I went from being an exceptionally confident little girl who loved to show off her talents and was always a leader to a bland member of the pack. I just stood by and watched as they tortured and bullied other little girls. They even forced one girl to change schools.

I told myself that because I wasn't participating in the bullying and that I had no control over it, but deep down, I knew I was wrong. I knew I should have stood up for those little girls. The old me would have stood up for them. I was just so focused on keeping my secret and being accepted that I let them down.

My own fear of being different stopped me from being myself. The old me that was trapped inside would have jumped in front of a moving train to save a stranger, but she was locked so far away, under layers of insecurities, that she had been rendered useless to the friends that actually needed her. The playground at school didn't feel like it fit me anymore. My friends didn't feel like friends.

4

THE SHOW MUST GO ON: FINDING COMFORT IN ACTING AND MUSIC

Being a "Working Actress"

As a kid, I became really good at compartmentalizing my life. My hearing issues were separate from my home life, which was separate from my school life, which was separate from my professional acting career. I had layers. I somehow found a way to be successful in one aspect of my life even when I felt like I was completely failing at a different aspect. I am going to take a step back and let you get to know the dreamer I was, even while I was fighting to hold onto what hearing I had left.

When I'd had my acting epiphany at the age of four, my mother had known I was serious. She had known this wasn't just a passing fancy. She had seen the conviction in my eyes as I gathered my family together at Christmas and made them all watch me perform. I sang along with Judy Garland, Broadway musicals, or Disney movies and danced my little heart out.

Granted, I was still a terrible dancer, even for a four-year-old, but she knew the love of performance art was there; she had seen it before. See, before my mom became pregnant with me, she had been an actress. She'd graduated from the Los Angeles Academy of Performing Arts in Hollywood, California, and even taught drama to kids in the Walnut

Valley Recreational Department for a few years. She had already gone through the struggles of being an actress.

It wasn't a profession her family was very fond of at the time, but she had followed her heart. She wanted to give me and my dream as much support as she could. So, she started calling agents, arranging for my first headshots, and teaching me how to slate my name (getting a four-year-old to stand still and say their name to a camera is even harder than it sounds, FYI).

Soon, my mother found an agent she felt believed in me as strongly as she did. Her name was Mary Grady. She owned the Mary Grady Agency, and she became like another grandma to me. She made sure to ask me what I wanted, which made me feel very grown-up. My list included things like a McDonald's commercial, a Barbie commercial, and to be on the Disney channel.

To this day, I still sometimes stop myself randomly in front of a mirror; recite, "Hi! I'm Amanda McDonough from —— and you are watching the Disney Channel"; and pretend to draw the Mickey ears. They both agreed that, if acting started to feel like work to me or if I stopped having fun, they would not push me to go any further.

AMANDA MARIE McDONOUGH

Amanda's first acting headshot.
(PC Schultz Brothers)

My first audition was for a national Honda commercial. I was so excited! I walked in all confident and friendly with a big smile on my face, ready to wow the casting directors. And wow them I did. I booked it! I was merely five years old, and I had just booked my first official acting job. I was on top of the world during filming.

I loved the attention, I loved the cameras, and I even loved the repetition of performing the same scene over and over again till it was perfect. Life on set felt like home to me, and I took on auditions with the same happy confidence that had won the first one and continued to book various commercials and a guest star appearance on a popular '90s television show called *Unsolved Mysteries*.

Picture taken on the set of Amanda's first TV show appearance, Unsolved Mysteries.

Discovering Live Performing

My first time performing a musical on stage was when I was in first grade. I was cast as one of the orphans in the play *Annie* at my elementary school. I still remember our little dance to "It's the Hard Knock Life" with white rags. I discovered, during this particular play, that while I was not very skilled at memorizing choreography for ballet, tap, or jazz class, I was great at musical theater dancing.

It was all about moving with the story, which is a concept that didn't quite resonate with me when I tried any other forms of dance. I loved being on stage and getting immediate feedback from the audience. It was heaven!

When I was in sixth grade, the school had auditions for the school play, *The Music Man*. I landed the lead role of Marian Paroo. I had held small roles in the previous school plays, but this time was different. I got to be the star! This was the greatest thing that could have happened to me at a time when my self-confidence was nearly zero, and I was starting to believe that my hearing loss would hold me back from doing the things I wanted to in life.

The play ended up being a family affair. My brother costarred as Winthrop (my character's little brother ... irony much?). My mother was recruited by the school to direct the play (because of her theater background). My father even pitched in as the videographer, capturing the whole performance on VHS—yes, VHS; I am that old. For those of you who are scratching your heads, VHS tapes were those big black brick-looking things with two rolls of film in the middle that ancient people used to record and watch movies. Anyways. Some kids would have hated having their family so involved in their after-school activities, but I thought it was cool that my family was so supportive.

Andrew as Winthrop and Amanda as Marian Paroo.

When I got up on that stage, the pain, fear, and uncertainty of my everyday life all melted away. I memorized my lines and recited them with my shoulders back and my head held high. I hit my stage blocking with deadly accuracy. I even nailed the choreography for all of the dances. Yet none of that impressed anyone.

They seemed to expect these things from me; after all, I was technically a professional actress. What blew them away was my voice. I had the voice of a little angel. I rounded my vowels, focused the sound forward, and used my diaphragm to support the notes naturally.

At one point during a dress rehearsal, our elementary school principal was walking by and heard me singing "Goodnight, My Someone." When she entered the room, she looked stunned and swore that she'd thought it was a CD being played. I recall her telling the story to anyone who would listen.

Until that point, I had only ever sung Spice Girls' songs on the playground with my friends. I knew I didn't have a terrible voice, but

I didn't realize that I was actually good. So, when I found out that my next adventure, middle school, had a school choir, I immediately signed myself up. I wanted to learn; I wanted to perform; but, most of all, I wanted to be heard.

Stealing the Spotlight

In a few short years of life, between the ages of four and seven, my brother had proven himself to be absolutely brilliant. Not only was he remarkably intelligent for his age, he also was unbelievably successful. You see, when he was four years old, after seeing me on television, he decided that he, too, wanted to try his hand at acting.

Like me, he started booking jobs almost immediately, but instead of them being commercials or appearances on TV shows, my brother started booking full-length animated Disney movies. His high intelligence and calm demeanor made him the only four-year-old in the business who could not only sit still in a recording studio for long periods of time, but also memorize his lines and follow directions.

Disney saw his brilliance after hiring him for his first small role in *Mickey's Once Upon a Christmas* and continued to hire him again and again for more of their animated films— including *Peter Pan II: Return to Never land*, *Lady and the Tramp II*, *The Jungle Book 2*, and *Finding Nemo*.

Voiceover work suited him, and before I knew it, my living room was filled with standing movie theater cutouts from his latest movies, my dog (who my father only let me keep for six months) was named after a character from one of his films, and the walls of our house were decorated with pictures of Andrew in the recording studio.

His life became quite glamorous, with red-carpet movie premiers and interviews. My accomplishments began to fade into the background. I started referring to our living room as "the Andrew Shrine" at school.

Part of me was a little jealous, even though the other part of me was extremely proud of him.

As Andrew grew up, he got straight A's without studying, and everything just seemed to come so easily to him. Everything he tried he was good at—music, art, poetry, soccer, karate, academics, acting, and on and on. We developed a bit of a rivalry. I would set the bar with my accomplishments, and soon after, he would shatter the bar with his.

He was smart and talented, and he could hear. Even though I was also intelligent, motivated, and talented, things always seemed to just happen for him, where I had to work hard and fight tooth and nail for the same achievements. This didn't make me love him any less, but it did affect our relationship as brother and sister.

The McDonough family—Julie,
Joe, Amanda, and Andrew.
(PC Schultz Brothers)

Singing

When I arrived at my first day of middle school, I learned that choir was literally the only thing I had to look forward to. Middle school was basically the equivalent of my own personal hell. Puberty had not been kind to me. I had thick dark eyebrows that still touched slightly in the middle because my mom wouldn't let me tweeze them. I had put on weight. My hair was frizzy like Princess Mia from *The Princess Diaries* (I'm talking the before picture, not the after). The uniforms we were forced to wear—khaki pants and a navy blue polo shirt—could not have been less flattering on me. It definitely didn't help that, for one of the two years I was there, I sported braces.

I wasn't even smart enough to go with the classic metal mouth look. I got clear braces that would get dyed weird colors whenever I ate something with food coloring in it. Welcome to the wonder years, folks.

Within the first few weeks at this new school, karma had caught up with me, and all of my elementary school friends abandoned me in one foul "mean girl" swoop. It was almost impressive how it only took the leader of our friendly group a couple class periods to convince every friend I had made since kindergarten to abandon me.

I remember walking my lunch tray to our designated table and having every girl (in perfect choreographed unison) stand up and move to a new table. When I innocently stood up and followed them to the new table, they then again stood up and moved back to the original. I got the hint.

I was no longer a member of the group. I was on the outside looking in. Middle school girls are mean. It wasn't a surprise really. For the last several months, there had been prank calls, jabs, teasing, exclusion, and passive-aggressive torture methods directed at me that had not escaped my notice.

Luckily for me, there were a few good Christian associate student body girls who allowed me to sit with them until I got back on my feet. They gave me "mean lessons" at lunch in an effort to teach me how to stand up for myself because I had fallen into a habit of always saying yes and letting everyone walk all over me. They were kind. But even though I was allowed to sit with them, I wasn't one of them. I was in so much pain I wasn't even "one of me" at the time.

This was all on top of all the "normal" teen pressure of a new school, new friends, and being forced to face the reality that my hearing had taken a significant drop. For the last several years, I had been "forgetting my hearing aids at home" or hiding them in my backpack after I got to school. Now I was stuck wearing them just to function in my classes. It would be safe to say that, from a preteen perspective, my life officially sucked.

My salvation came in the form of the one-hour choir class I got to take each day and a band of misfits obsessed with things like *Lord of The Rings* and *Harry Potter*, who became my new best friends.

Every day I would enter the choir room and let out a long breath filled with all the horrible events that had already happened to me that day. I could let go of the guy behind me in science who casually referred to my ears as "Dumbo ears" or the moment when the cheerleaders waved in my direction and I happily waved back, not realizing I was standing in front of the jock table.

I felt pretty invisible until the moment I entered the choir room and took my seat, safely among my fellow altos. Then, as our choir teacher took her place on an elevated platform on the front of the room with a music stand as her podium, I would discretely turn my hearing aids off and stuff them in the front pocket of my knockoff JanSport backpack (not even a knockoff of the cool one everyone else had, a knockoff of the one with too many pockets to be cool).

I didn't like to sing with my hearing aids on. They made the sounds around me feel electronic and made it nearly impossible to blend my voice with the singers around me, as my hearing aids were always magnifying the wrong sounds in the room, not giving me a real sense of the balance of the voices around me.

So, into the deep, dark pocket of my backpack the hearing aids went every day for an hour. When the bell rang and everyone started grabbing his or her backpack to leave, I would discreetly slide my hearing aids back on and go about my day. No one ever noticed because no one ever looked. I learned in middle school that people only see what they want to see. To the adults I was a healthy-looking young girl. There was no reason for them to suspect there was anything different about me. To kids, I was a choir geek or a nerd. Everyone around me was so caught up in his or her own life and his or her own problems that keeping my secret had become almost easy.

Background Acting

On top of not really fitting in at school, my acting career had come to a staggering halt. At the time "awkward preteen" wasn't a popular television character. Unlike some lucky stars, puberty wasn't helping me live up to Hollywood's beauty standards; I wasn't getting any auditions, let alone booking any roles. I told myself I was "focusing on my academics" to try to make myself feel better, but it wasn't the truth. Hollywood didn't want me anymore.

I wasn't happy in middle school—not that anyone is ever happy in middle school; but I was miserable. There was no theater program, no opportunities to act, and the art and choral programs had limited resources. It bothered me that lots of kids in these classes were just taking the classes for credit instead of actually being passionate about expressing themselves creatively.

This changed the vibe of the classes for those of us who actually needed to express ourselves this way. I felt trapped. I missed acting, and since I wasn't getting any auditions, my mother decided to sign me up with a kids' background acting company.

She figured that, at least this way, I would get to be on set and surrounded by kids who had the same interests and drive as I had. I started working the background both in real life at school and on television. I worked on some big-name shows like *Zoey 101, Hannah Montana,* and *Living with Fran* (where they bumped me up to costar to play an awkward Jewish teenager).

I got to meet some big-name actors and make great money for a thirteen/fourteen-year-old. Some days, I even worked with my brother. I remember one specific time on set. He and I were both working background on a commercial, and he had just gone through a growth spurt. (I, however, had basically stopped growing in fifth grade.) So he and I were the same height and looked about the same age (despite me being four years older than him).

A woman walked up to us between takes and asked us if we were twins. When we replied with a firm no, she looked disappointed (twins are really valuable in Hollywood). I worked one day here and another day there. There were teachers on set. Every time I worked, I got to miss school. It was great!

On set, I felt more comfortable with myself. Each day, I got to start from scratch. Each day, I made a new group of friends and spent my day getting to know them better. If I didn't like them, tomorrow would bring new friends. And this made it even easier for me to hide my hearing loss because no one ever got close enough to me to get to know who I really was.

Working on set again helped me start building up a little more confidence, which I brought with me back to school. People love self-confidence. As a result, I started making more friends there toward the end of my eighth-grade year. At this time, I was working regularly on the film *Christmas with the Kranks* starring Jaime Lee Curtis and Tim Allen. I actually almost missed my eighth-grade graduation ceremony because I was booked to work on the film that day.

My mom had to put her foot down and straight-up told the AD (assistant director) that her daughter wasn't missing her graduation and that we would arrive on set as soon as the ceremony was over. Sometimes, stage moms can be as sassy as dance moms. I made it to set just in time to start filming our first scenes—thanks to my fellow background kids' ridiculously long hair and makeup requirements. I think we may have given that AD an ulcer though.

My two years of junior high were an adventure. I worked, PE sucked, I had to start wearing bras for the first time, and I got my first period. Somehow, I magically managed to make it through junior high with only minor bloodshed and a fantastic GPA. Not everyone is so lucky.

High school performing

High school could not have come fast enough for me. The school district had built this brand-new high school on the hill adjacent to the one my house sat on. I could literally see school from my backyard and hear the bell ring from my living room. I had mixed feelings about it.

The building had won all these architectural awards, but honestly, it was made completely out of cement; it was gray and cold—which made it perfect for films, commercials, and music videos. The district would rent the school out to films on weekends. Films like *Die Hard* (there are so many of those, I honestly don't remember which one exactly) and *Serenity* were filmed on campus. But it felt a little like a prison for those of us actually attending school there during the week.

Yet, I will admit that it was kind of cool to be able to say your high school was used in car commercials, Disney channel music videos, and big blockbuster movies whenever you ran into someone from a rival school.

Even though the school was brand-new, half of my classes were in portables behind the multilevel school building. We didn't have a regulation football field. And the school's version of a stage had a garage door that opened and closed, allowing it to be used for storage.

It wasn't ideal, but it was so much better than middle school. Here the arts were taken more seriously. There were two award-winning choirs at my new high school, and I had to audition for them during the summer between middle school and high school just for a chance to be a part of them. I was so nervous for my audition. I went with a group of my friends from our middle school choir, and we all held hands and practiced with each other as we waited our turn.

The choir teacher was a woman of pure class and beauty. Her hair was always up in a bun, and she looked almost more like a ballet teacher than a choir teacher. She was intimidating but kind at the same time. Just being in the room with her, I knew I was going to learn something.

Most of my friends and I made it into her all-women's choir. It was an advanced choir but not her most advanced. There, we learned the art of blending, vocal techniques, how to read sheet music, and music history. Through the course of the year, she challenged us to sing Italian arias, jazz, musical theater, modern music, and songs in Latin.

She exposed us to Bach and Mozart. She taught us how to feel the story in the music and to let the notes show us the way. I was learning so much from her and was so jazzed when I got my first solo. That solo was the confirmation that I belonged there—the confirmation that I wasn't just skating by but, rather, excelling. All of this was despite the fact that, every day, I came into class, and just like I had in middle school, I hid my hearing aids in my backpack to sing.

We had your typical high school drama club. You know, the kind of drama club where the same few people get the leads in every play. Where each year's play is picked based on what characters they play best. This doesn't suck if you are one of the "it" people. But it kind of sucks when you are on the outside looking in.

My friends and I joined as freshman, and we were in awe of the junior and senior members of the club. We had some incredible talent at our school. One of our drama club members even performed professionally in Cirque du Soleil during high school. A few more of those original drama club members went on to be very successful actors and performers after graduation.

When it came time for the school's musical, *Cinderella*, my friends and I auditioned with dreams of landing a starring role, but we were freshman and knew it was a long shot. When the cast list was posted, we eagerly ran to find out if we had made the cut!

Our fingers scrolled down the list as we each found our names one by one—ensemble, ensemble, ensemble, Chef #2. Wait, Chef #2! I had gotten a solo! I was so excited! Yeah, it seems kind of silly to me now, but I have to remind myself how fragile my self-esteem was and how withdrawn I had become back then!

My sophomore year, the spring musical was set to be *Once Upon a Mattress*, the more mature musical version of the classic story *The Princes and the Pea*, which originally starred one of my favorite musical actresses, Carol Burnett!

I was only a sophomore, but I wanted the lead role of Winnifred more than anyone knew. She was a loud, obnoxious, ungraceful amazing character. With this character, I would have to completely let go of every one of my insecurities and go all out. I showed up to auditions ready to give it my all.

I totally blew it. In the middle of my audition, I forgot the words of the song. I didn't stop singing for a second though; I made up words as I went along, focusing on not breaking character. After the audition, I was distraught. I was beating myself up for "failing" in my audition.

For days, I mentally tortured myself, until the cast list was finally posted on the cold gray wall outside of the choir room, putting an end to the uncertainty of it all. To my surprise, and everyone else's, I got the lead role. I was only a sophomore, and I was going to be Winnifred!

Our little garage door stage wasn't made for proper theater productions, so we used the stage at the Pomona School District building. It was an old stage in desperate need of some updates. We had to bring our own lighting and sound equipment and set it up for each show we did there.

Wires ran across the floor of the first several rows of the audience, held down by tape so that no one tripped. Large speakers atop metal poles blocked the views from several of the seats as well. Sometimes the microphones that were clipped to our collars and wired down our shirts to a mic pack clipped to the back of our costumes worked. Sometimes they didn't.

Rehearsals were long, but the hours and the art brought us all together as a family. There was a small green room just off the side of the stage with three mirrors, a couch, and some sinks that hadn't worked in probably fifty years. Everything about the building was outdated.

But then there was something about that smell of the old wood of the stage, the look of those dusty red curtains as they strained to open, and the squelching every seat made in the audience as it was lowered to be sat in that made me so happy I thought I would burst.

Opening night, I put on the curly auburn wig, adorned with branches and leaves sticking out of it in disarray. I sang and danced my heart out on that district auditorium stage. The play was great! Everyone loved it, and I did a pretty great job, if I may say so myself.

To this day, that is my favorite play I have ever performed. Nothing made me feel more alive than stepping into a new character, forgetting my own troubles, and feeling the butterflies dance around in my stomach as I took my first steps out onto that old wooden stage. The lights blinded me as I made my way to my mark and introduced the audience to my character as I belted the first note of the song "Shy."

High school was going pretty good, until tragedy struck. Well, it wasn't a real tragedy but a drama club tragedy. It was met with the same reactions as if the school had caught fire and we were all trapped inside (which actually happened a couple times thanks to the potheads who liked to smoke on the hillside and would catch the brush on fire every once in a while; but that is a different story).

Our drama teacher was leaving the school, leaving our drama club with no teacher supervisor, which meant that our club would lose its chartering!

We panicked. When I told my parents, they talked about transferring me to Diamond Bar High School, which had a real theater with up-to-date lighting, sound equipment, and an established theater program. Yet the thought of leaving a school I had just become comfortable with, where all of my friends were didn't appeal to me.

I teamed up with a couple of friends, and we figured out how to get the club rechartered. We found a new teacher supervisor, we launched a fund-raising campaign, and we made it happen. Not bad for a small group of drama nerds. As a reward for my efforts, I was voted drama club president—a title I am still proud to have held.

During my junior year, the school hired a new drama teacher. She was actually the wife of my favorite English teacher at the time. He was a character, with his bow ties and platform clown shoes. She was a character too, with her red hair and boundless energy.

Yet I was anxious to learn more and do more. I longed for more theater training than public school could offer me. I decided to look into some professional children's theater companies to continue my theater education. I wanted more of a challenge.

I started working with a professional children's theater called the Royal Theater Company on its production of *Annie*. There were two casts, and in both casts, I had a different lead role. My favorite was Lilly St. Regis, though I had gone into auditions wanting the role of Miss Hannigan more than anything.

I had separate instructors in dance, vocals, and acting. I learned a lot in a very short period of time and finally got to perform on a real professional stage, where I didn't have to help set up the lighting and sound equipment! Then, a few days before opening night, I got laryngitis.

I couldn't sing, I could barely talk, and I was terrified the company would give my role away. I had worked so hard with my instructors for this performance, and I refused to miss it. I was put on vocal rest before the show—which, at the time, was basically a legalized form of torture for me. I was a talker, and not being allowed to talk was devastating!

I showed up at my call time, and then there was the moment of truth. "Try to talk," I was instructed. I hesitated for a moment, afraid that nothing would come out, that I would fail my cast mates and myself. Then, after a beat, I opened up my mouth and said my first line with clarity. Everyone applauded backstage. I headed into wardrobe and makeup, practicing bars and warming up my voice. The show went on with me, not my understudy.

On that professional stage, I felt invincible. School was a bit more challenging though. Between losing our beloved choral teacher, who left to start her beautiful family, and having a hard time adjusting to a new drama teacher, my friends and I were frustrated. We desired, more than anything, to be educated in the arts; we thirsted for it.

The string of substitute teachers in our choral classes, who had no music background and made us do music theory notebooks all day long, were not cutting it. We started sharing techniques and learning from each other. We tried being creative outside of class, but we felt trapped.

Since I was working with the Royal Theater Company on *Annie*, I decided not to try out for the spring musical at school, *You're a Good Man, Charlie Brown*. I was still drama club president; when I discovered that the play had no stage manager, I stepped up and took on those responsibilities.

Anyone who knows anything about theater knows that a show cannot go on without a stage manager. Stage managers are given the least amount of recognition, yet they are in charge of lighting, sound, props, sets, cues, and the curtain (basically everything except the acting and directing). Everyone had a blast, and I developed a long-standing respect for anyone brave enough to be a stage manager.

I measure high school in school plays and moments—not in classes or in years, but by how many times I got to be on stage. Let me explain. I had some really great teachers in high school, I learned a lot in my classes. I did well on my SATs and had outstanding grades. Those experiences didn't define me as much as my experiences in choir and drama did, though.

I still had enough hearing left in my ears to do the things I loved, so I did them every day. I loved singing, dancing, and acting. Participating in these activities with my classmates kept me happy and excited about going to school. I feel for kids going through the education system now, where arts programs are the first things to disappear with the budget cuts. I wonder how they will measure their high school experiences.

My final high school play was the same as my first play ever—*Annie*. When I was five or six years old, I had played an orphan in our elementary school play. My second experience with the play was with the Royal Theatre Company portraying Lily St. Regis. This time around, I was finally going to be playing the ever-so-coveted role of Miss Hannigan!

I still remembered being on my elementary school stage and standing in a line with about ten other kids singing "It's the Hard Knock Life" while I waved a white rag around with the beat. This time, I would be the one striking fear into those young girls' hearts. It felt like my life of student theater education was coming full circle. It was a poetic way to end my high school acting career. My brother even had a role in the show, like he had back when we'd performed *The Music Man* when I was in sixth grade.

In the theater and music aspect of my life, I had it together. I was the lead in the school plays; I had wonderful artistic friends who would constantly break into song and dance with me; and I performed at school events like football games, assemblies, and rallies.

Because I was constantly on stage singing, talking, and bringing characters to life, no one suspected that I couldn't hear. It was the best cover anyone could have come up with to hide my "secret identity." The arts gave me an outlet for the pain I was privately suffering; they allowed me to be someone else for an hour or two, to feel something besides anxiety and fear.

That was something I needed desperately, as my hearing continued to decline and everyday things began to become more and more challenging.

5

ADAPTATION OF THE SPECIES: ADAPTING TO HEARING LOSS

Emotionally

Teachers can have a profound effect on their students. Most of the teachers that left a lasting impact on me as a teen didn't leave it because they taught me how to take a test but, rather, because they demonstrated something to me about life, made me feel something strongly, or taught me something in a way that kept me interested in it for longer than the time it took to take the test.

I was still a nerd, so I was very focused on grades and test taking, but I was also at a point in my life where I was malleable. Who I would become was being shaped and molded by the people in my life.

I had this teacher my freshman year of high school. He was probably in his late twenties or early thirties at the time. He taught science, was very handsome (like Superman meets Elvis handsome, with the strong chin and the swept-back dark hair). He was the first person I remember meeting under the age of sixty who had hearing loss.

I was only fourteen years old, so to me he was still "old." Therefore, I didn't really identify with him, but he was the first person I had ever seen be upfront and honest about his hearing loss. Our first day in Bio, he explained his issue with his hearing to our class.

He had a slight accent that I couldn't place but later found out that it was a common product of growing up hard of hearing. He too had tried his hand at acting before becoming a teacher. He was best known for the line, "Yes! Another one for Jesus!" from some movie he was in.

All his students would try to make him say it every chance we got! Even the mean kids who mimicked his accent outside of class and tried to take advantage of his hearing loss had to admit they liked him. Even though it was comforting knowing he existed, knowing of just one person living openly with hearing loss wasn't enough.

I can't tell you how many times I just wanted to walk up to him after class, show him my hearing aids, and have him tell me everything was going to be all right, though I never did. That secret had become a huge part of my life. I was at a new school trying to figure out exactly who I was. I didn't want to be known as the hard-of-hearing girl or let that define who I would become in high school. So, my secret stayed a secret.

Now that my hearing was starting to really affect my school and social life and my hearing aids were becoming a mandatory everyday accessory, I started to feel more alone and anxious about my secret. I watched TV and saw no one I could relate to. I flipped through magazines and saw beautiful people who don't have to worry about their hearing.

I went to the movies and watched stars communicate effortlessly with one another. There were no hard-of-hearing role models for me to look up to in the media at all. If they did exist, they were doing a great job of hiding from me.

Marlee Matlin (whose work was still too mature for me to have any exposure to) and Helen Keller were the only deaf people anyone around me had ever heard of. I didn't know sign language, and I wasn't mute or blind, so I didn't really relate to them. I didn't want to be limited. I didn't want to become "disabled."

I didn't want to be pitied or looked down upon. I didn't want to be seen as a second-class citizen. I didn't want to be deaf or hard of hearing. I just wanted to be me. Those fears that used to cause me to fall asleep crying at night crept back into my head. What would happen to me if I did lose any more of my hearing? What if I never heard my mom's voice again?

What if I could no longer use a phone? What kind of job would I be able to hold? Why would any guy want me? I had no one to show me what my future could be like or how to function as a deaf person. Could I even be successful if I was deaf? My future felt so uncertain.

The uncertainty grew to the point that I became afraid of dreaming. What if I lost any more of my hearing and couldn't act anymore or sing? My backup plans at this time were becoming a doctor or a teacher. Yet I believed that, if my hearing got any worse, I wouldn't be able to hear my patients or my students and, therefore, wouldn't be allowed to teach or practice medicine. I was terrified, to say the least, of an uncertain future that may or may not happen.

Conversations

Being a teen with moderate hearing loss wasn't easy or enjoyable, but I had lived with hearing loss for as long as I could remember. I had spent years gradually adapting my brain and body to doing things differently to offset the disadvantages I had as a result of my hearing loss.

I studied people's body language to gauge how to react to situations and sentences I couldn't hear or understand. I used the observation of the hearing people around me to be alerted to things like when class was over, if an alarm was going off, if an emergency vehicle was nearby, or when a phone was ringing.

I came up with at least thirty different ways to say, "What?" or to ask someone to repeat what he or she had just said. I would oftentimes stealthily change the subject to avoid asking someone to repeat him or herself. This allowed me to control the content of the conversation so I could listen for key words and gauge mood from facial expressions.

When all else failed, I would change the subject by making fun of myself, calling myself a ditz, or telling people I was just easily distracted by shiny objects. I used humor and an innocent smile to hide my embarrassment and anxiety over the fact that I was struggling to communicate.

I began to notice myself staring so intently at people as they spoke, focusing 100 percent of my attention on their faces, that I started making some people uncomfortable as a result. I didn't know it at the time, but I was actually unconsciously doing some lipreading to help where I couldn't hear.

I also had adapted to controlling my environment. When we would have to do group projects, rather than meet at a restaurant or coffee shop or somewhere random, where sounds were unpredictable, I would reserve controlled study rooms in the library for group meetings or host them at my home.

I would take charge and be the leader so that I could delegate any tasks that required hearing (phone calls, interviews, and the like) to my group members and sit at the head of the table during group meetings. That way, I could see everyone and know when each person was talking.

In class, I always sat in the front row, on the right side so that the teacher and the rest of the class was on my left side, aka my good hearing side. I would even slightly cheat my desk and/or my body to the left, so that I could see and hear anyone asking questions in class more easily.

If I lost my place in the book, I would look over to see what page my neighbor was on. If I couldn't understand a movie playing in class, I would start discussing it with one of the smart students once class got out. I would ask them their opinions on the film, what they thought would be on the test from the film, and secretly sneak in questions to clarify whatever parts I hadn't heard.

People love to talk and be asked their opinions on things, especially AP students. I never had any trouble getting the information I needed from them.

At home and on my own time, I would read ahead in my text book, Google (or Ask Jeeves) questions I did not have the answers to, watch YouTube videos (or rent videos from Blockbuster) to visualize any topics I still didn't understand, and read articles on real-life applications of the principles I was learning in class. I worked ten times harder than any other student I had ever met. While my peers were going to parties, raves, or concerts, I was studying.

At the end of my senior year, I started to notice my hearing loss was getting worse and that, as it did, the amount of time I spent talking exponentially increased. My gift of gab started out as a blessing, causing me to make lots of new friends who would mistake my willingness to share my stories and opinions with them as confidence.

But it quickly became a curse. It started off as a cute, quirky, Zooey Deschanel-type nervous banter. People found it adorable and endearing. Yet it quickly turned into a fierce inability for me to simply shut up, which was a problem, because apparently people actually like it when you take the time to listen to them.

Yet this was my defense mechanism. I was struggling so much to understand what was being said to me that it was easier if I didn't let others get a word in edgewise. Some people found it hilarious, others, annoying.

I didn't do it on purpose. I was so unbearably terrified of not understanding what a person was saying to me that I would just start talking and couldn't easily stop. Honestly, even though I have spent years working on listening more and speaking less, I still to this day sometimes find myself going off on never-ending tangents. I can't help it.

When I get nervous, I talk. Usually, I talk about the most random things possible, spurting out little known facts, obscure movie references, and terrible jokes. It is incredibly embarrassing but has become a part of my personality that people close to me have learned to live with. In high school, I could tell it was starting to annoy my friends, but I didn't quite know what to do about it. I tried to hold it together and count down the days until graduation.

In Class

Like every teenage girl in the early 2000s, my white, clear-sleeved binder was covered in pictures of boys—Legolas and Cedric Diggory to be more precise. I don't think I actually grasped the concept of "celebrity" crushes appropriately. I was more in love with characters from books, but this was my life.

I had gone from hanging with the cool girls on campus in elementary school to being a full-out nerd—drama nerd, book nerd, and choir geek. I belonged to quite a few awkward high school social classifications but none that were stereotypically considered popular to belong to.

The only problem with being a nerd in honors classes with hearing loss comes when you realize that your new math teacher has a thick accent, your assigned seat in his class is near the back of the room, and he spends most of the class time writing on the whiteboard with his back to the class, therefore directing all the sound he is producing into a wall.

I went home each night and read ahead, but reading math in a book made no sense to me. I needed to see the progression, how the numbers evolved and interacted, to understand. So, after I got my first C ever on a quiz, I went to my mom for help. She quickly hired me a tutor, and things started getting better again. I was still behind in class, but at least I had a resource to help me catch up.

Dated

I never have been lucky in love. I went through a few minor crushes in high school, but I've always been a loyal person, so I somehow managed to crush on the same guy from kindergarten through my senior year of high school. The crush ended abruptly the day he decided to make out with a random cheerleader in the backseat of a van that I was also in with a group of our friends.

During their passionate backseat wrestling (for lack of a better term), my high school crush and the random cheerleader kicked me and my best friend (who were the poor souls stuck in the middle seats of the van directly in front of them) in the back of our heads. It's safe to say that crush ended, leaving me to mourn the twelve years of my life I had wasted pining over a guy who was actually a huge jerk.

My taste in guys didn't get better my senior year when I started dating this guy from our school play. At that point in time, I still hadn't had my first kiss. I was playing the role of Bianca in the Shakespeare play *The Taming of the Shrew*. Bianca has a kissing scene, and even though our director had agreed to not make us actually kiss in rehearsals, we were going to have to kiss on stage. I was devastated. I didn't want my first kiss to be on stage. I wanted it to mean something. I was also superembarrassed that I still hadn't had a first kiss. I was almost eighteen years old, practically an adult.

I started talking to the guy who played Petruchio in the play. We talked every day after school on the phone, and one day, he asked me to grab food with him after rehearsal. I did. We had a great time, and he invited me to go golfing. I thought things were going well, but apparently the lack of physical intimacy after two dates was a problem for him, because one night, not long after we finished talking on the phone, he "hooked up" with one of my best friend's sisters in the backseat of his car.

When his recent hookup bragged to her sister about the conquest, her sister texted me to let me know. I was heartbroken. I couldn't help wondering if guys would always turn out to be like this one and my kindergarten crush.

The two of us obviously didn't work out. My first kiss was awkward and wet. It happened on a stage during dress rehearsal for *The Taming of the Shrew* with a guy I barely knew. At least he seemed to be as weirded out by the whole situation as I was. The stage stole my first kiss, but at least I didn't give it away to someone who didn't respect or appreciate me.

Naturally, I was determined to bounce back and have an outstanding date for my senior prom. I wanted the fairy tale—the guy asking me out with some cute sign, the dress shopping with my friends months before prom, the whole deal.

The guys at our school disappointed me. As prom started to draw dangerously close, I still hadn't been asked by anyone. I was beginning to fear that I would have to go alone. My mom encouraged me to tap into my inner feminist and just ask a guy to the prom myself.

Just before prom, I had returned from a school educational trip of England, Ireland, Scotland, and Wales. I had gotten to know this cute guy who went to our school while we were abroad. He was younger, but I decided to ask him if he would go.

He said yes! My prom dreams were revitalized, and I started spending my free time cutting dress ideas out of my *Seventeen* magazines. And then he approached me only a week or so before prom and told me he couldn't go anymore.

I was back to square one, and my pride was a little damaged. Nevertheless, I was determined to go to prom with a guy—any guy. So I made a list of guys who didn't have dates, would be cool to hang out with, and would look good in my prom pictures (yeah, I was a little vain).

I decided to ask a guy I had known since elementary school. I thought for sure he would say yes so close to prom, since he didn't have a date. He said no, his reason being that he couldn't afford it. Everyone knows this is just a nice way of saying, "I want to go but not with you."

He was nice about it, but the rejection hurt. Yet again, I went back to the drawing board, all this time putting off dress shopping because I still didn't have a date. As a last-ditch effort, I asked my friend's brother. I thought he would say no because he was kind of a punk rock, "don't care about those stupid traditions" type, but to my surprise, he was actually eager to go with me.

I picked out a last-minute dress. I had been holding off because I firmly believed that the dress should match the date. It was a white strapless A-line with these black and silver polka dots on one side of it. My brother called it a Cruella de Vil dress, but I thought it looked kind of like a more contemporary Cinderella.

It felt like it went with my date to me. The prom ended up being awesome. My date was a lot of fun, and there wasn't any of that weird teen sexual pressure you hear about on TV shows and such. We went, we danced, we hung out, and we had a good time.

Amanda before her senior prom with her date
(far left) and her friends (2008).

6

DENIAL IS A GIRL'S BEST FRIEND: NOT ACCEPTING MY HEARING LOSS

Growing up with hearing loss wasn't all negative. It taught me how to think outside of the box, how to come up with creative solutions to problems, and how to persevere.

I was lucky to grow up with supportive parents. The best thing they did for me, as a "hearing impaired" kid, was they never used the word *can't* in our home. I was raised to believe I could do anything if I put my mind to it and worked hard enough. I was never given any slack because of my "disadvantage;" I was expected to work hard and do well in school, socially, and in the arts.

My hearing loss was never an acceptable excuse for not trying something or for failing at something. Because I never heard the word *can't* from my parents, I never used it myself. *Can't* wasn't in my vocabulary. Though I knew everything in life would always be harder for me, I still believed that I could do whatever I put my mind to. This is one of the gifts growing up with a challenge like hearing loss gave me.

Though I lived a very sheltered and privileged life with my stable happily married middle-class white family with a roof over my head, regular family vacations, plenty of food on the table and no financial stresses, being a kid who couldn't hear saved me from the naive belief that life would ever be fair. Life hadn't been "fair" to me since I was four years old, and it only got harder every single day that passed.

This helped me build up resilience and instilled in me an understanding that life owed me nothing. I was entitled to nothing. I needed to be grateful for everything I had today because it wasn't guaranteed to me tomorrow.

In Denial

It took me years to appreciate any of these lessons, though. In my youth (wow that makes me sound old), I was in denial. I worked so hard to "act" like I could hear that, as the years passed, it became harder and harder to break character and figure out who I really was.

The benefit of "playing hearing" was that it caused me to never hesitate to try to do something my hearing peers wouldn't think twice about, such as auditioning for a solo in choir, or even simply joining choir. Had I let my hearing dictate my life, it would have been all too easy to say, "I have hearing loss. I can't audition for choir because it will be hard for me."

I still held onto that promise I made to myself when I was four years old. I kept that secret and carried the burden on my own. I still believed that, if people didn't know I was different, then they wouldn't treat me any differently, and I would no longer be different. A part of me even still believed that my hearing would stabilize and stop getting worse and worse.

I refused to talk about my hearing loss. I refused to use phrases like *hearing loss, hearing impaired, hard of hearing,* or the dreaded *deaf.* I didn't want to be associated with anything that had to do with not being able to hear like everyone else. In doing so, I was keeping everyone who wanted to be close to me at an emotional distance to protect my denial and my delicate psyche, but at the time, I didn't care.

I became an overachiever. To satisfy my deep-seated denial, I felt I had to be the best and excel at everything. I had to get straight A's, I had to be the lead in every play, I had to get that solo, I had to join the most clubs, and I had to make everyone like me. I had to be perfect.

I had to convince everyone that I was okay and that there was nothing wrong with me—even though inside, I felt lesser than my peers. I felt like I was not quite human but, rather, something incomplete. I thought that, if people knew I was broken, they would discard me like rubbish. So I made myself look as flawless on the outside as I could. It was exhausting.

The crazy thing is that I wasn't unhappy. I had lots of friends, great grades, pride in my accomplishments, and confidence in my talents again. I just couldn't accept the one part of myself that wasn't okay. I couldn't accept that I couldn't hear.

I was actually so far in denial that I compartmentalized my life. The hearing tests every six months and continual doctors' appointments as my hearing continued to decline were separate from everything else in my life that I loved—school, theater, choir, performing, friends, family, and singing.

I did this so much so that my brain actually physically filed it differently. All of the bad, stressful, embarrassing, or painful memories related to my hearing problems basically got blocked out in my everyday life. In order to remember them or recover them, I would have to make a serious conscious effort. It is almost like I found them too traumatizing as a kid and my brain blocked them out, allowing me to feed off of the happy memories instead of the bad ones.

Stubborn

I was also stubborn. I never asked for help or accepted help. I was determined to do everything on my own. I was determined not to ever owe anyone anything. Any success I had, I wanted to know that it was because I had earned it and deserved it. I needed to know that I was able, capable, and strong.

I was so afraid of this deaf stereotype, this idea that people who cannot hear are frail, sickly, old, disabled, and unable to be independent and support themselves. I was determined to do everything I could to be the opposite of the stereotype. I needed to prove to myself that I was capable of being successful on my own.

However, this hurt me in a lot of ways. It caused me to push a lot of people away. It also caused me to miss out on a lot of opportunities, simply because I wasn't willing to ask for help or allow others to contribute their diverse viewpoints, ideas, and talents to my work.

By only relying on my own limited knowledge and life experiences and keeping my hearing loss to myself, I probably missed out on a lot of great resources and information that could have made my life with hearing loss easier at the time. But I wasn't ready to accept that my "hearing impairment" was a part of me. I wasn't ready to be vulnerable. At this point in my life, I needed to be strong to survive.

My senior year, my mom somehow convinced me to take sign language as an extra elective. At the time, though, I didn't feel passionately about the language or the topic. That was probably because I was still trying so hard to distance myself from anything hearing-loss related. I was so deeply in denial that the class and language scared me, even though it should have been something that helped me.

American Sign Language should have given me access to a new way of communicating and my first peek at deaf culture. Instead, the only two words I committed to memory in sign language were *cute* and *boy*, to be used in exactly the context by a straight teenage girl that you would imagine. I wasn't ready to allow my hearing loss to become a part of my identity.

Relationships

In high school, there was this opportunity for honors and AP students to go to Italy on an EF educational tour, and I just had to go! I was raised in Italian American culture with a loud, large, loving family.

My mom's maiden name was Amicangioli, which, in Italian, means "friends of the angels."

The members of her side of the family truly lived up to the name. They are some of the kindest, most selfless, most wonderful people I have ever met. I wanted to go to Italy to get to know my roots and also to hang out with my friends in a foreign country (mostly the latter though).

Two of my best friends, Jen and Chelsea, had already committed to going on the Italy trip, and I was determined to go with them. After I'd spent hours, days, and weeks of begging and doing research on how experiencing cultures and history firsthand can help with child development and education to present to my father, my parents finally said I could go! Not without thoroughly guilting me about how much it would cost. But I got to go, so I was psyched!

It was, without a doubt, one of the best experiences of my young life. It also proved to be an eye-opening one. Right before we left for Italy, I had another drop in my hearing—a hearing drop that may not have been noticeable to my parents but required a new adaptation for me.

On the outside, I was seeing historic buildings, having the best time with my best friends, and eating gelato and margarita pizza every day. But secretly, I was struggling to hide my hearing aids from my roommates. I was unable to understand our tour guide, Mario, through his thick Italian accent as he pointed out historical landmarks our charter bus passed.

I was unable to effectively communicate with the locals. And the audio tours that narrated the museums as we walked through were nearly useless to me. It was like listening to an out-of-tune radio. The words were there but drowning in a thick accent, distorted, and hard to make out most of the time.

I could gather enough information to form a basic outline of what the voice-over recording was talking about but struggled with the details. I made the most of it though; I read description signs wherever they were available, I had my close friends recap information for me when they could, and I managed to still enjoy nearly every new experience on that trip.

Well, there was the exception of my first encounter with espresso. It turns out espresso and I don't mix well; apparently it stains porcelain skin and clothing if you choke on it and spit it out (just FYI).

I had gotten to nearly James Bond status about hiding my hearing aids from the people I spent twenty-four hours a day with; it was almost creepy how good I was. The application of my hearing aids every morning looked simply like I was brushing my hair behind my ears.

No one suspected a thing, until one morning when I was rushing to get downstairs in time for breakfast. Instead of stealthily slipping my hearing aids out of my bag, hooking them over my ears as my fingers pushed the hair back, and then closing the battery door as I slid the hair back over my ears in one swift motion, which took less than two seconds (yeah, I was that good), I messed up.

Jen, my high school best friend, who I affectionately called Pooh Bear, caught a glimpse of my hearing aid. I had been caught red-handed! My spy days were over, and my secret was out. I did my best to explain to her that I was hard of hearing and had been hiding my hearing aids from the world for as long as I could remember.

I begged her to keep it a secret, and being the great friend she was, she agreed. My secret was no longer just my secret. It felt kind of nice to have someone to talk to about it. We spent nearly every moment together, and Jen started noticing things. She started catching on to when I was not understanding things Mario said on the bus and repeating them for me.

Jen started helping by explaining the history of some of the buildings we were touring that had audio guides to me. After the tour, she became kind of my lifeline during interactions with locals.

We were teenagers and boy crazy. We played a game as we toured Italy where we all tried to find the hottest Italian boy in any given city, and whomever could get a picture with the most attractive Italian man by the end of our trip won bragging rights.

I was too shy and too self-conscious to get any pictures, but my friends were definitely not. I envied them a little their ability to just go up and talk to people, never having to worry about whether or not they would actually hear or understand a stranger.

That doesn't seem to be something that people who grew up with normal hearing worried about. It is something that plagued my thoughts. Every single one of my failed human interactions motivated me to simply avoid interactions with people wherever I could.

When we returned from Italy, I knew things were going to change. Jen knew my secret, and anyone who has ever read the book or watched the show *Pretty Little Liars* knows, "Two can keep a secret if one of them is dead." I was afraid that, now that one person knew about my hearing loss and my hearing aids, everyone would find out, and it would be like an atomic bomb blowing up in my face.

I was afraid everyone would start treating me differently. I was worried that everyone would hate me for keeping a secret from them, and everyone would abandon me. I was prepared for the worst that first day back at school, but nothing changed.

The day went on as it normally did. Jen didn't press me about telling anyone, and she kept the new information to herself. If anything, life got a little better. As time passed, Jen started picking up on physical cues that I gave off—like changing what side I was standing on during a conversation or the way I slightly leaned in and squinted a little when I was having a hard time hearing someone or the way I laughed when I had no idea what was going on.

She used to tease me for having two laughs, the first laugh when the joke was told and then my second laugh when I actually understood the joke.

She started knowing when I needed help, and without me asking her, she would repeat parts of sentences that she noticed I missed. She would look at me when she talked no matter who she was talking to so I could hear and see her.

She began sitting and walking on my left side (my better hearing side) so I didn't have to turn to hear her. If I looked lost or confused, she would even covertly repeat the topic or main points of a conversation so that I would be caught up. She was my guardian angel. As school went on, I started to take her help for granted a little. I also started relying on her a little too much.

The two of us were basically attached at the hip. We were involved in almost all the same extracurricular activities. I hung out before and after school with her. I even managed to get a bunch of the same classes. People would joke that Jen was my keeper. She would even get blamed whenever I did something wrong. I think it bothered her a little sometimes that I would get so much attention.

She wasn't the only one who discovered my secret. By junior year, I found out that my close friend Chelsea had known for a while. She never treated me any differently for it. Actually, I remember one time when she had a pool party and one of the boys picked me up and was about to throw me in the pool. I quickly ripped my (not waterproof) three thousand-dollar hearing aid off my ear and threw it to her.

She caught it and hid it under a towel until I was able to get out of the pool. That's what I call a good friend! I had spent so many years pushing people away and keeping them at a distance so they wouldn't find out about my hearing that I never realized that there might be some people who could help me and be on my team.

7

THE PURSUIT OF NORMALCY: TRYING TO LIVE A "NORMAL" LIFE

I remember the day I turned eighteen. I had been stressing about college applications, upcoming AP tests, making sure I had enough volunteer hours and extracurricular activities to make myself attractive to colleges, and my SAT tests. High school was almost over, and I had no idea what my future was going to look like. I didn't know what college I wanted to go to or what I wanted to major in. It was all a little overwhelming.

The morning of my birthday, my mom had made me a special breakfast, and the kitchen table was covered in beautiful brightly wrapped presents that she had bought to make my day memorable. I remember my dad nonchalantly coming out of his room while I was eating; patting me on the shoulder; and saying, "Happy birthday. You are officially an adult. Get a job." He walked away with an amused grin on his face.

Finish high school, choose a college, find a major, get a job. I listed the steps in my head. I knew in that moment that being an adult was not going to be as fun as they made it look on TV.

Graduated from High School

My heart nearly leaped out of my chest as I heard my name called at my high school graduation. I walked up the stairs thinking to myself, *Don't trip ... don't trip ... don't trip,* as I received my diploma and took my picture. I had just graduated in the top ten of my graduating class.

The top ten of us got to sit in a special box. We didn't have to wait for our names in alphabetical order, so instead of waiting forever for the M's to be called among my huge graduating class, my parents got to hear my name called at the very beginning of the ceremony.

Cords and ribbons representing all of my club memberships and extracurricular activities weighed down my shoulders. I also got to sing "Remember Me This Way" with the other choir graduating seniors at the commencement ceremony. It was a beautiful day filled with sounds of joy and laughter and happiness. We had made it!

Pregraduation with Jessica, Jen, Alicia, and Michelle.

Get a Job

Before graduation, I had decided to fill out job applications for a great summer/college job. Growing up, I had been blessed to have a family that could afford annual passes to Disneyland. My dad and I used to go on Sundays and watch the bands together at Tomorrowland Terrace.

I would sing along, and my dad would play air bass as we bonded over the music. Disneyland seemed like the perfect place for me to start working after high school. I already knew where all the bathrooms were anyway. I applied as an attractions operator and learned a few days before graduation that I had gotten the job!

Anyone who has ever worked for Disney will tell you that the company culture is out of this world. When you first get hired, they have a way of sucking you in. Walt Disney becomes your role model, and Mickey Mouse is referred to as your boss. The perks of being a "Cast Member" and the amazing people I got to work with made it the perfect college job.

Disney has this uncanny way of attracting the best people. While I was working there, I made lots of friends—friends that I will have for life. I met people I will always admire. I made memories that I wouldn't trade for the world. It wasn't all perfect. I remember working in the pouring rain without shelter and my skin burning in the intense California summers without shade for a very tiny paycheck.

Yet, this job was exactly what I needed in college. It taught me a lot about organization structure, and hierarchy; how to improve efficiency, maintain safety, and foster positive company culture; California regulations; company pride; and a good old-fashioned hard day's work.

Julie McDonough and Amanda McDonough
in front of the attraction "The Golden Zephyr"
inside Disney's California Adventure Park.

College

Picking a college felt nearly impossible. I had no idea what I wanted to do with my life. At the end of my senior year of high school, I had done a program at Pomona Medical College for kids interested in future medical careers, and I had loved it! Yet the thought of being a doctor who couldn't hear felt wrong to me. I was terrified my hearing would make me misinterpret something a patient said, and I would not treat him or her properly. It was too much responsibility.

College applications were stressful. My father encouraged me to check the disability box on them, but I refused to do so. As a result, I received no financial aid opportunities, even though my outstanding grades, kick-ass personal essays, and extensive extracurricular lists got me accepted into almost every college I applied to.

Not having any financial aid options limited my choices

significantly—down to two possible colleges. I still had a passion for acting and singing, but my father insisted that I get what he considered a "real degree" as a backup plan. I saw the practicality in this and agreed. I looked to see if any colleges offered film programs, but the ones in my price range didn't.

So, I settled on business as my major. I figured that I could use knowledge in business no matter what I decided to do with my life. After much debate, I ended up sending a letter of intent to California Polytechnic University, Pomona Campus, (Cal Poly), my father's alma mater.

I decided to be an overachiever and pursue a bachelor of science in business administration, double majoring in international business and marketing management, with an emphasis in entertainment marketing. Yeah, you try saying that five times fast.

I knew my parents wanted what was best for me, and they were paying for my education. The least I could do was save them money by living at home and going to school down the street at Cal Poly. At the time, I wasn't completely satisfied with my college choice though.

I always dreamed of this Hollywood-esque college experience. I wanted to study abroad, join a sorority, act in college plays, join clubs, live on campus, and go to football games. None of those things ended up happening though. Cal Poly was a commuter campus, and a majority of the institution's students were working their own way through college; most didn't have time to get too involved on campus. I was no exception.

I was working while going to school. Even when I tried to make this "idealized college experience" happen for myself, things got in the way. It just ended up seeming like it wasn't meant to be. I attempted to join the school plays, but no one I talked to (and I talked to a lot of people) could tell me how to audition.

I tried to join a coed business fraternity, but my hearing made it impossible to get through the interview process (and made me look like a clueless idiot in a stadium classroom filled with frat members asking me questions I couldn't hear in the large room that echoed).

I tried to join clubs, but my part-time job left me no time for club meetings, and I had no financial aid to afford studying abroad. Yet I did have straight A's in my classes. I loved being able to make my own schedule, and I was making a few friends in my classes as well.

It may not have been the college experience one sees in Hollywood movies, but it was the perfect experience for me. You aren't going to get those typical crazy college stories you would expect in this chapter. Actually, my college life was pretty much PG-13. I had the best first two years of college ever! Ironically, I owe a lot of those great college moments to my job.

In college, my time was divided between classes, work, the thirty-minute-to-an-hour-each-way commute to and from work, studying, and attempting to have a social life. More of my time was spent at work than at school. I developed some strong bonds with my coworkers.

Every night, the group of us who closed the park would clock out of work together and drive down the street to the local Denny's. There we would eat, laugh, and share our stories from that day. We were all in our teens and early twenties, just kids going to school and working part-time.

We all shared a love for the theatrical, Disney characters, and food. Keeping my hearing loss a secret had become second nature to me. I wouldn't have even known how to tell a person I was hard of hearing if I had wanted to at this point in my life. It didn't stop me from being able to do my job, and I was certainly able to make friends; my hearing aids stayed tucked beneath my hair as I went about my day, transitioning from student to commuter to coworker to friend.

Campus was beautiful. It had rolling green hills, horse stables, and farming areas. There was a giant facility building that reached up to the sky and came to a strong point, towering over all other buildings in the area and visible for miles. My classes were fun and challenging.

I loved the quarter system. Having only a handful of weeks to complete a class kept me on my toes and ensured I wouldn't get bored or lose interest in the material. Learning made me feel strong; it gave me a sense of purpose. Working made me feel independent and in control of my life.

At work, I was taught to put the needs of others first, to anticipate those needs, and to do little things that made a difference (like pick stray trash off the floor, hold doors for strangers, and greet everyone with positivity and a smile). These things became habit and eventually a part of my personality.

I even managed to land my first boyfriend. I was living on top of the world! I liked who I was, I liked where I was in my life, and I knew exactly what I was working toward. These were the "good old days." Very few times in my life have I experienced such balance. It was the calm before the storm.

Amanda in front of Cal Poly
Pomona. (Chelsea Mundy)

The Girl in the Band

During college, my access to music continued to gradually shrink, but I refused to give it up. Maybe that refusal was out of fear of another loss, maybe it was pride, or maybe it was determination. Whatever the case, I kept right on singing in my shower and in the privacy of my car.

My father has played the bass for as long as I can remember. He was such a lover of music that he even had a recording studio built onto the back of my childhood house with special soundproof walls. He filled the room with sound mixers, amps, microphones, and basses. He used this room to rehearse for his band performances and to record my brother's voice-over auditions.

When I was in elementary school, he would put on *The Phantom of the Opera*. I would sing Christine's lines, and he would sing the Phantom's lines as we danced around (me on his toes). My mom was always writing her own songs with her acoustic guitar, and my brother was basically a child prodigy on the piano. You could play any song for him off of a CD or MP3 (yes, that is how old we are; this was the ages before the iPod), and after about thirty minutes, he would be able to pluck it out on the piano.

He was superimpressive, since he had never taken a single piano lesson. My whole family connected through music. As we grew up, my mom would have my brother and I perform at family gatherings. I would sing, and he would play the guitar.

Not long after high school, my mother convinced me that I should audition for *American Idol*. I spent a week just trying to pick the right song. At the time, my favorite genres to sing were jazz and blues, which are not very *American Idol* audition friendly.

My mom talked me into calling my old choir teacher and singing my selection for her over the phone to get her notes on my performance. I practiced my butt off for this opportunity. The day of auditions was insane. Almost ten thousand people filled the Pasadena Rose Bowl seats, with numbers pinned to our shirts indicating that we were auditioning.

The participants were accompanied by their supporters. Some brought friends with them; some brought family. I brought my mom. Some people came dressed in eccentric clothing to grab the judge's attention. Everywhere you turned, there were people warming up, touching up makeup, and fixing hair.

We had all been asked to learn a song by the singer Pink, which we sang in our stadium seats as several cameras scanned the crowd. My mother kept me calm and made friends with the people around us as we waited hours and hours. She encouraged me at hour four and continued cheering me on in hour six.

If not for her, I would have definitely left after hour two. Finally, my number was called (along with a group of many others). Only the performers were allowed to the audition stations spread out along the stadium. They herded us like cattle into lines on the football field grass.

These were just the initial auditions, so none of the famous judges were there. There were little tents set up on the field filled with producers, assistant producers, and the casting directors. They hurried us into smaller lines and rushed through each audition like it was a fast food drive-through.

On my turn, I took a step up to the line (aka tape on grass) and slated my name. I then sang my song just as rehearsed. The judge looked at me for a second and then asked me why I was auditioning for *American Idol*. I could have given her this amazing sob story about how I was losing my hearing and was afraid this was my last chance to fulfill my childhood dream of being on *American Idol*.

Actually, that truth probably would have gotten me on TV, but I think, if I had told it, I would have always wondered if I had gotten there because people felt sorry for me or because I had real talent. My secret remained a secret and I gave her some generic "because singing is my passion" type of response (which was also true). Two seconds later, she yelled, "Next!"

I didn't make it past the first round of auditions, but I still considered it an accomplishment that I even had the guts to go or the patience to wait all those hours just to audition.

When I entered college, my voice sounded more mature and trained. It was then that my father asked me if I would be interested in being a backup singer in his band. That was the single highest praise I'd received from my father to date. Being asked to join him in the one activity he cherished above all else was beyond an honor.

It was validation that I had done something so well that my father was proud of me, which, due to his cold military-type demeanor, is something he would never actually say out loud. I excitedly accepted his invitation, and before I knew it, I was in the band!

The band consisted of a group of guys in their forties and fifties, all with stable jobs in corporate America who nevertheless got together once a week to make music. Our repertoire consisted of the greatest hits of the '70s and '80s, and it kind of rocked. They were all really talented men who had chosen a life of stability, education, and family over their rock star dreams but had never lost their love for music.

I was learning so much about performing from them. I loved it! After proving myself to them at the first few rehearsals, they gave me my own songs to sing lead!

My dad and I kept my hearing loss a secret from them. My dad would adjust his bass amp so that it faced directly at me because the bass was the one instrument I had no trouble hearing (or feeling).

Sometimes my ears would lose the notes of the lead singer, guitarist, pianist and occasionally the drums, but the bass was always there for me. I got most of my cues from my dad's playing; luckily for me, he never messed up. If I messed up, he would make sure to let me know so that I could fix it for the next rehearsal.

I still remember our first real gig. It was in a bar in Fullerton, California, not far from Disneyland. I am not even sure I was old enough to drink at this point, but there I was up on that stage with my dad, his band behind me and our lead singer next to me. The bar was filled with our friends, family, and patrons. I remember my first solo song, Aretha Franklin's "Respect."

It's not an easy song, but my voice was made for belting. I started it with my eyes closed, focusing my ears and my entire being on the music as the intro played. Once I heard my cue, my mouth opened, and out flew the first few notes. When I opened my eyes, everyone was dancing, my mom had a proud look on her face as she filmed the song on my dad's camera, and my whole body was filled with happiness. That was a great gig. I had worked so hard, and all that hard work paid off.

Amanda sings, and her father, Joe, plays the bass during a gig in a bar in Fullerton, California.

8

BYE, BYE, BYE: WAKING UP DEAF

The Decline

As time passed, I started struggling to hear the phone over the large crowds at work. I held my free hand to the phone box and relied on the vibrations of the phone to tell when it was ringing.

It turned out lots of the older cast members also struggled with this; I requested (for them of course) that a light be put in the top of the closed metal boxes containing the phones to give us a visual alert when the phone was ringing. The request was unfortunately ignored, but it was one baby step toward me one day being able to ask for help for myself.

I had been promoted a few times since I'd been hired. Now, as a Guest Control Lead, I wore a walkie-talkie so that I could be called upon wherever I was in the park and to make communication easier. At first, I loved it! It made me feel important. But the sound quality and background noise (we were communicating in a theme park, so it was always loud) made me strain to understand the speakers.

I asked people to use the text feature when contacting me because I was managing up to twenty employees, handling guests, and maintaining safety during loud parades, making it hard for me to answer their calls or even hear them. (No one questioned my ability to hear with this request because everyone had issues communicating with the walkie-talkies at some point.) Unfortunately, no one actually used the text option when trying to contact me. So I got creative.

When you have hearing loss and you love your job, you really need to be able to think outside the box and come up with unique solutions to your unique problems. My solution to the walkie-talkie problem was to mentor my employees. Each day, I would pick a "shadow," someone interested in becoming a lead in the future. I would teach the person how to set up the parade route, how to manage a crowd during a show, and how to answer walkie-talkie calls.

This practice boosted the morale of my cast members and made them eager to work harder, in hopes they would get picked to shadow me the next time they were assigned to me. This relieved me of the stress of trying to hear mumbled calls with lots of background noise. It was a win for everyone for a while.

It may have just been a part-time college job to many, but I took my job seriously. I loved making people smile, I loved who I worked with, and I loved what I did. I think everyone should work a service job at some point in his or her life. Yeah, I got yelled at and mistreated by guests quite often, but it taught me the true value of kindness and to never believe myself to be "better than" or superior to anyone. We are all human.

The day my hearing had decreased to a point where I felt that, in the near future, I would no longer be able to do my job safely, I put in my two-weeks' notice. After nearly three years with the company, I said goodbye and clocked out of my last shift. It broke my heart to have to give up on anything because of my hearing, but I respected my job and the safety of others too much to continue.

I told my friends that it was just time for me to move on, but deep down in the pit of my stomach, I had this morbid feeling that an end was coming, and it absolutely terrified me.

After I left Disney, my life changed drastically. Another drop in my hearing caused me to go from someone who relied on hearing to communicate—even if it was just a few syllables and my mind connecting the dots using body language, vocal inflections, facial expressions, context, and the length of the words to put together sentences like a puzzle—to not being able to depend on my ears at all.

My human interactions were so embarrassingly one-sided that I felt the need to start explaining to people that I was "hard of hearing." I was still afraid of the word *deaf*. I had been raised in a culture that pitied those who identified as deaf. I was raised to think that the deaf couldn't be independent, hold jobs, or communicate effectively.

I didn't know how to explain my hearing loss to my work friends. With the exception of a chosen few, they all believed me to be a "normal" hearing person. How could I explain to them that I now had severe hearing loss? To my friends, it would feel like it had happened overnight, but for me, it had been a daily struggle for as long as I could remember.

I felt lost, confused, and displaced. I didn't want anyone to see me at less than my best. I broke up with my boyfriend of nearly two years when I realized that my future was going in a different direction than his. What direction that was, I had no idea.

Between no longer being able to understand his slight accent and beginning to isolate myself from everyone who knew me before this new decrease in my hearing, I let him go. I left my old life and old Disney friends in the past. I did this partially to preserve the memory for myself and partially so my friends there would remember me as I was, not as who I was becoming.

Losing My Voice

One day I went out with my girlfriends, Jen and Michelle. Michelle drove. The two of them sat in the front, and I sat in the middle of the backseat, leaning my body forward so that my head was between theirs so I could hear them. A new pop song came on the radio.

They turned it up so that the entire car shook with the bass, and they started belting the words of the song as we drove through Chino Hills.

The three of us laughed and moved along with the music. As the chorus approached, they jumped in and sang in unison words that I realized, in a single moment of horror, I could not hear.

The words were gone. My ears did not pick up a single lyric. I could hear (and feel) the bass, the drums, the guitar, and the mumbled sound of a voice; the actual words were completely missing. It was almost as if the singer herself had forgotten them and, instead, was just belting random notes unintelligibly.

I wanted to cry in that moment when I realized music would never be the same, when I realized that I had lost another battle with hearing loss. Instead I held in the tears, bobbed my head up and down with the beat, and slowly sunk back into the backseat of the car, attempting not to alert my friends of the change in my mood as I did so.   In an instant, I went from feeling happy and carefree to feeling devastated.

Not long after, it was my singing voice that disappeared. My band would play, but no matter how loud I turned up my mic, I simply couldn't tell whether or not I was singing the right notes.

My singing days came to an abrupt and painful end, causing me to leave the band. I'll always cherish that year with my dad and his band. My hearing loss had stolen another precious thing from me—my dream; a passion; and, worst of all, a huge part of my relationship with my father.

The day I quit the band was the end of an era. My relationship with my dad would never be the same. It wasn't because he was angry with me—he knew I had held on as long as I physically could—but because we no longer had music to bring us together.

Singing was my stress reliever. It was how I expressed myself. It made me happy. And it was something that I was really good at. I used to talk about singing on Broadway, but the day I lost the ability to hear my own voice, that dream died. As time passed, my speech started to deteriorate. My words started to jumble together, and I started regularly mispronouncing things.

I used to have a bookshelf in my room by my bed filled with CDs. I owned every type of music, from Beethoven to NSYNC. Those CDs became too painful to look at when I could no longer enjoy music. One day, I grew so angry that I threw them all in a yellow bag; walked into my dad's home recording studio; and said, "Here, I never want to see these again." I left that bag at his feet and walked away without looking back.

I still had some hearing. I still could understand some peoples voices; the deeper the voice the easier it was for me to hear. I could still hear the bass and, most of the time, the drums. But things were getting harder and harder for me. I didn't know what to do.

The Hail Mary

Hit with a sudden inspiration to take back my life, I woke up one morning and decided to make the most of whatever amount of time I may or may not have left with my hearing. I acknowledged that the end of my life with hearing might be near, and I started running.

I took up actual physical running because I decided that, if I only had a short amount of time left to hear, I was going to spend that time doing what I loved most—acting. And in order to be a successful actor, I needed to drop about ten pounds (yeah society's beauty standards are whack, and I subscribed to all of them).

With a dream revived, I had purpose again. I was determined to adapt and use any means necessary to achieve my goal. In my head, once my hearing was gone, any chance of me ever being a well-known actress was gone too. After all, there was no one like me with hearing loss in the media spotlight, no one to look up to, no role models I identified with, and no one to show me the way. I guess I was always destined to make my own way in this life and to pave my own path.

Like most things in my life, returning to acting wasn't easy. I started submitting myself for roles and going on auditions, but I felt self-conscious. I was so afraid of not being able to understand the casting agent, and that insecurity bled into my audition performances.

Sometimes my nightmares were realized. I couldn't understand what the casting directors were saying to me or asking me to do, and I reacted like a simpleton. I was losing the weight, which helped me get more audition opportunities. Without confidence in yourself, though, how can you make others feel confident that you are the right choice for the job? My "Hail Mary" attempt at making myself successful before that D-day my gut kept telling me was coming was a flop.

About a Boy

It was the summer after my junior year of college with one more year to go until I finished my degrees. I dated a bit that summer, made some new friends, and attempted to maintain some form of normalcy. I started spending a lot of time with the boy next door, a hard-core geek who lived with his parents.

He started joining me on my runs, which became walks to accommodate all of the talking we did. Every day for an hour or two, we would walk in the hills surrounding our homes and talk about everything from philosophy and literature to religion and *Star Wars*; no topic went unexplored.

He was easy to talk to. For some reason, I understood him. I struggled in conversations with everyone else around me, but when he spoke, my brain registered everything crystal clear, like magic. He was the first person, since my high school best friend, with whom I could open up about my hearing loss. He quickly became my new best friend. I could tell him my darkest thoughts with no judgment, my strangest fantasies, and my outlandish hopes. With him, I felt safe. With him, I felt like I could truly be myself.

We spent every possible waking moment together. He wanted more, though. Every time I had a date, he would say, "Don't go out with him. Go out with me." I would laugh it off, and we would continue our conversations as if he'd never said it.

Eventually, he wore me down and I gave him "one date to prove that I should be dating him." He didn't disappoint. He picked me up in his car, opened my door, took me to a gorgeous restaurant with amazing food, ordered me my first chocolate soufflé for dessert, and treated me like a princess. To my surprise, it wasn't awkward. Conversation flowed easily like it always did, but the candlelight added a little something magical to the way I looked at him. So we started actually dating.

They say the best relationships start as friendships, and I felt like everything with us was going wonderfully. I felt like I had finally picked a good guy! I was incredibly happy, even though my acting career still wasn't going anywhere, I didn't have a stable paycheck coming in, and my hearing sucked. Being with him and dating my best friend made all my other troubles seem smaller somehow. It was almost like knowing that I had someone to face these challenges with took some of the burden and pressure off of me.

I will never forget the day he got sick. I think it was laryngitis. Naturally, I took care of him—brought him pre-prepared restaurant soup (which is near impossible to find in the middle of a 90 plus-degree California summer) and kept him entertained as he focused on his recovery.

I always had an awful immune system, so I knew there was a good chance I would catch whatever he had, but I didn't care. A few days later, I was sick, and he was healthy. He left the week I got sick for a trip out of town with his friends. He formally asked me to be his girlfriend right before he left. I was thrilled. That night, I went to sleep not knowing that, when I woke up, everything would be different.

It was a deep sleep; I have always been a good sleeper. It is one of my greatest talents. I can sleep anytime and anywhere. This particular morning, I awoke and knew something was wrong. I awoke to complete and utter silence—a silence and stillness that any person with a tiny bit of hearing could not even possibly imagine. I was officially, profoundly *deaf*.

At first, I panicked. I tried knocking loudly on things. I tried yelling. I tried hearing anything. But it was all gone. I sat down at the edge of my bed, staring at my reflection in my full-length mirror as the sun came up in the window behind me, and to my surprise, the young woman looking back at me smiled. I suddenly was overcome with an overwhelming feeling of relief. I was *deaf*, and I was relieved.

Now, some of you may think this was temporary insanity, but it actually wasn't. I had spent my entire life living in fear. I'd spent my entire childhood afraid of one thing—silence. I had gone to bed every night praying to God to save me from the silence. Now silence was here, and I was free.

I was free of the fear. The worst thing I had ever imagined happening to me had officially happened, and I was fine. I was still breathing. I still had the same thoughts. I still retained the same knowledge. I was still me but void of sound.

When you have hearing, there is always sound—even if that sound is limited to the background noises your brain naturally tunes out. There is always a car passing, a bird outside the window, a dog barking down the street, or even just the sound of your own beating heart and breath entering and leaving your lungs.

People with even the smallest amount of hearing are never alone; sound is always there, like a friend holding your hand through life, warning you of danger, and helping you connect with others. Well, that morning, my friend left me for good. A piece of my body, my being, a piece that had been suffering and struggling and holding on for twenty-two years finally passed away.

Naturally I wasn't happy about becoming totally deaf, but it wasn't what I had always thought it would be. I'd always assumed it would be the end of my world, but here I was, still alive and kicking.

If this had been the only tragedy to befall me that week, I think I could have handled it with at least an ounce of dignity or maybe even with some grace. But if you have been reading since the beginning, you know that my life is never that simple. No one's life is. Life doesn't just sit there and say, "Oh well, she already had one big thing happen to her this week. I'll give her a break." No, life piles it on and tests us in the cruelest ways. That is how life makes us strong.

My boyfriend had been back in town a few days but hadn't come to visit me, which was odd. I needed to talk to him. I needed my best friend to comfort me and tell me that everything was going to be all right. I needed him to tell me he didn't see me any differently now that I was deaf. I needed to know that the people closest to me would still see me for me, not the pathetic "disabled" person I'd always feared I could become.

When my boyfriend finally did come to visit me, he wouldn't come in my home. He looked upset when he sat next to me and started explaining something. I had a hard time understanding what he was talking about. The only words I managed to clearly decipher of his long explanation were, "I cheated on you in San Francisco." Everything else was just a jumble of lip movements. I was devastated. My heart sunk, my head was spinning, and I felt sick to my stomach. He wasn't only my boyfriend. He was by best friend. And he had betrayed me. At some point in the conversation, he said the girl's name, but to my knowledge, he never actually broke up with me. He seemed repentant. So, I foolishly forgave him, and we kept dating, only for me to learn a few weeks later that he was leaving me for her.

He packed his bags and followed her to another state—leaving me without a boyfriend or a best friend at the one point in my life when I needed support and acceptance more than anything. I spiraled. I was hurt. I was lost. My self-esteem was shot. For the first time in my life, I experienced hate. I hated him and for a while, I blamed him for my whole life falling apart. The hyperbolic rug had been pulled out from under me, and I was left on my ass.

Tonsillectomy

I was filled with anger, anger that impaired my judgment and my comprehension of all the changes that were going on around me. To make matters more complicated, my body still wasn't strong. I was still very sick, and my doctor recommended I have a tonsillectomy to help prevent me from becoming ill so frequently in the future.

Once my body had healed from the illness I'd contracted from my now ex-boyfriend, my tonsillectomy was scheduled. I was a little nervous, since it was my first surgery ever. I had some concerns because my family had a bad track record with anesthetics, but the tonsillectomy went pretty smoothly.

I don't know what I was expecting when I woke up. Maybe somewhere deep inside my subconscious, I was hoping that, when the surgical team removed my tonsils, they would take my hearing loss with them. I think, since I still had been given no real explanation for my hearing loss, that I was secretly hoping my tonsils were somehow to blame and that everything would be all healed up when I awoke.

There was no such luck. Instead, the surgery had left me temporarily mute. I came out of the anesthetic to find myself still in complete silence and now with no voice. I was a deaf-mute. There was no denying the word *deaf* anymore. It was the only word left to describe my level of hearing loss, but the new descriptive word came with something else new—pity stares from everyone around me.

Loss

I was confined to the couch after my tonsillectomy, watching reruns of NCIS for ten hours a day. The only way my family could communicate with me, since I couldn't hear, speak, lip-read well, or use sign language, was through the use of a whiteboard I kept with me at all times.

They would write a question, and I would write my response back and forth until we understood each other. It was miserable. I felt trapped inside my own body. I couldn't express myself, I couldn't communicate, and I couldn't connect with my big loving family who came by one-by-one to check in on me during my recovery. I started to resent them.

I sat there silently in my spot on that couch, glaring at them as they happily talked and laughed in the adjacent kitchen. I could watch them, but I felt like I would never be a part of their world again. I felt alone, completely alone, marinating in my misery on that couch.

The only thing that took my mind off of everything was television. I could still get lost in the stories and the characters (with the help of closed captions on the TV). It was hard at first, finding a balance between reading the words scrolling across the bottom of the screen and watching the actual visual performance.

It was a challenge to read as quickly as the characters spoke. Sometimes I felt frustrated trying to keep up with the letters as they sprinted across the screen, flashing in and out with each line. I tried reading the character's lips, but the camera angle changed so frequently that I could rarely read a half a sentence before the shot on the screen switched to the opposite character's reaction.

I sat on that couch day in and day out feeling useless, hating that I couldn't connect with anyone, and wondering what I was going to do next.

When one is faced with tragedy, we are given two choices—find the light or dwell in the dark. Now, anyone who knows me (and I would like to think you are getting to know me pretty well by now) knows that I am stubborn. When I put my mind to something, I have to achieve it. There is this little flame deep in my gut that burns for that achievement. At this point in my life, that flame burned for one thing and one thing only—finishing my college degrees.

I had made myself a promise and there was no way I was going to let myself down. I had been through way too much to fail now.

I am only human; I was pretty bitter for a short while and definitely not a fun person to be around. But cut me some slack. My heart was broken. I was recovering from surgery. And at the same time, I was being forced to face something I had been running from for approximately eighteen years. That is enough to make anyone act like a brat.

9

LEARNING TO DEAL: I WASN'T PREPARED TO DEAL WITH DEAFNESS

Relearning the Basics

After lots of daydreaming and crying, I decided that I wanted to learn how to lip-read. So that's what I did. Since scripted shows changed angles too frequently, I used the news station to practice reading lips. The camera stayed fixed on the reporter. Even when it changed angles, the reporter's face was always visible. I used that to my advantage.

The captioning for the news was always absolutely terrible so that helped me not feel tempted to cheat in any way; there was no way to cheat. I either understood what was being said, or I didn't. It was like a pass-fail class. I was determined and continued to do what it took to succeed.

I also wanted to learn to talk again, since my speech had been deteriorating from lack of use and my inability to hear it to control it. Teaching myself to talk again was even more difficult than teaching myself to lip-read. Once my tonsillectomy incisions had healed, I started trying to make sounds again.

I would squeak and hum and buzz, but it was all just silence to me. I could feel my throat vibrating with every sound. I could feel a change in where the vibrations occurred depending on how high or low a pitch I was producing. I seemed to have the muscle memory of how to create sounds, but my words were mushed and unintelligible at first.

They all blended together, having no clear beginning or end. One night, in frustration, I lay down on my bedroom floor and began to cry. I turned over on my side to face the full-length closet mirror and take in the sight of the pathetic creature before me. To my surprise, as I watched the tears trip down the side of my face, I saw potential.

I sat up, scooted myself up close to the mirror and began practicing the way words were formed with my lips. I mouthed "hot–dog," "air-plane," "ice–cream," the same dreaded words that had been used over and over in my hearing tests since I was four to measure my word understanding.

I repeated these motions over and over and over again until I accidentally let out a noise. I jumped. The sound coming out of my mouth had bounced off of the mirror and reverberated right onto my body. I could feel it. It felt sudden, sharp, and strong. I tried making a soft sound.

It too bounced off the mirror, meeting my skin with a softer feeling. I had figured it out! This mirror was going to help me feel how loud or soft I was being and when I was making and not making sounds. Every day, I sat in front of that mirror overpronouncing my words and practicing being soft or loud.

I felt the vibrations and placements in my throat to tell if I was speaking strangely or normally. Every day, I got a little better; every day, I felt a little more confident.

My family didn't see any of this hard work; all they saw was me sitting for hours on the couch watching TV (aka lipreading practice and an escape from my reality) and me locking myself alone in my room at night (aka speech rehearsals). They didn't see the struggles, the frustrations, the tears when I failed, or the smiles when I succeeded. I have never been good at letting others see me struggle.

When I started speaking to them again and started having them use the whiteboard and pieces of paper less and less and talk to me more and more, they didn't really think it had taken too much effort for me to start interacting with them the same way I used to.

Now, my lipreading skills and speaking skills were far from perfect. I often didn't understand others, and they often didn't understand me, but I kept trying. My father would frequently stop me midsentence and make me repeat words that I had not spoken clearly or had mispronounced.

To strangers, it may have seemed rude, but I was grateful. If I was going to speak, I wanted to speak to the best of my ability, and in order to do that, I needed someone with working ears to tell me when I had messed up. I was still pretty bitter and upset, but at least now I was functioning.

Everyone Treated Me Differently

Despite how hard it was to teach myself to talk again and to lip-read better, those weren't the hardest things about my new life. The hardest parts were the looks of pity, the loss of independence, and the constant need for help. There was all of a sudden a long list of things I "couldn't" do.

I couldn't use a phone, schedule my own doctors' appointments, order through a drive-through, or talk to a stranger, to list a few. I started to worry about how I was going to function in my classes when fall quarter arrived, and it was coming quickly.

I had attended my first three years of college without any real assistance for my lack of hearing. I now had to find a different way to understand what my professors and peers were saying in class. This meant swallowing my pride, forgetting my stubbornness, and asking the disability resource center on campus for help.

It was strange to see the difference in how people perceived me now that I started identifying with my level of hearing. I liked to daydream about the first three years of college—a simpler time when it was easier to make friends and when people treated me well because they believed me to be just like them. I liked remembering that feeling of strength and independence that I felt I had before.

I didn't know how to function as a "deaf person," how to do everyday simple things without relying on hearing. I had relied on whatever hearing I had left to navigate every action and every interaction my entire life. Our society is incredibly sound dependent. Everything from our alarm clocks to simple human conversations depends on sound.

I had never really met a deaf person before. There were none on TV to learn from. I had no mentors to show me how to do simple things like knowing when someone is knocking on my front door without being able to hear it. I knew I had to figure this all out on my own. I couldn't do that in my parents' house with them constantly babying me and looking at me with pity.

I negotiated with my parents (yes, *negotiated* is the right word to describe the conversation we had) and convinced them that living on my own, right off campus, was the best thing for me right now. I didn't want to be dependent on anyone. The only real way to learn how to be independent is to take a flying leap and just do it.

I moved into a two-bedroom apartment with three other girls right across the street from my college campus. I had watched so many college TV shows and films that summer while I was stuck on that couch that I think I had built up this fantasy in my mind that my roommates and I would become best friends, take a road trip across the United States, meet the perfect guys, and have brunch together every Sunday after we graduated until we were old (screeching record sound).

That so didn't happen. Nevertheless, I can't ever say my senior year wasn't eventful, thanks to those roommates.

Life on my own was hard. It really tested my creativity. I feel I need to remind you that I didn't have any deaf friends or access to information within deaf culture that could tell me how to do simple things like wake up at a certain time in the morning, know when someone was knocking at the door, or know when I was slamming cupboards.

That was actually one of my roommates' pet peeves about me. I was always slamming the cupboards and doors in the morning. I wasn't doing it on purpose mind you; I had simply forgotten cupboard doors make noise and couldn't gauge how loud I was being.

I also was terrible at cleaning my dishes (which had nothing to do with my hearing and more to do with being used to having a dishwashing machine). Other than that, I was a pretty great roommate. My roommates could be as loud as they wanted as late as they wanted, and it never bothered me.

To solve all those "simple" problems, I came up with a few interesting solutions. When I knew someone was coming over, I would literally sit in front of the door with my back touching it, feeling it for the vibrations of someone knocking and staring out the peephole every three seconds to make sure I didn't miss the knock.

This was not a great solution to my problem. It also made me seem a little weird to my roommates and guests and caused me a lot of unnecessary anxiety. I knew there had to be a better way; I just didn't have anyone to help me figure out what that was.

To wake up on time, I would set the alarm on my phone, set the phone to vibrate, and fall asleep with the phone in my hand. So, if I end up with hand cancer when I am older, we all know why.

I never really found a solution to the cupboard problem though. No matter how hard I tried to be quiet, I was always loud.

My loudness wasn't limited to cupboard and door closing either. I had no volume control on my voice. Half the time, I spoke too softly for anyone to hear me, and the other half of the time I spoke way too loudly, to the point where I would embarrass my roommates or classmates, and they would shush me. It was mortifying.

I got lucky with my roommates. They were pretty accepting people.

I could have done way worse. They didn't baby me, and they didn't talk down to me. No roommate is ever perfect, though. Two of my roommates were huge social butterflies. They constantly had guys and friends going in and out the door.

I was a bit of a homebody, so I was usually there when their guests arrived. They would introduce me to their friends with a, "This is our roommate, Amanda. She is *deaf*! She actually reads your lips!" To this, each of their guests would react with looks of surprise or awe as I said, "Nice to meet you."

Then every single one of them felt the need to "test" my lipreading skills. "Tell me what I am saying!" they would proclaim, followed by them overexaggerating the words *olive juice*, which is supposed to look similar to *I love you*, or with the word *watermelon*.

I don't know why 99 percent of them chose one of those two words to test me, but they always did. The other 1 percent would use this as an opportunity to hit on me by saying things like, "You look cute," or "Hey girl!" It started out with me feeling flattered that everyone seemed to be so impressed with my lipreading skills, but it quickly turned into me feeling used.

My roommates had turned a skill I relied on to survive and communicate into a cheap parlor trick to entertain their friends. It started to feel degrading, so I began hiding away in my room when they had company.

Now it wasn't their fault. They didn't know better, and I didn't have any experience explaining my hearing loss to people, so I didn't know how to tell them.

My three roommates weren't always around though. The girl who shared a room with me slept at her boyfriend's nearly every night, so I had my room to myself 90 percent of the year. My other two roommates both moved out halfway through the year.

For about a month, until they found new students to place in the second bedroom, I had the apartment completely to myself. This was not exactly the fun college experience I had in mind and came with a few scares. Remember how I told you I would stand by the door and wait to feel people knock when I knew to expect company?

Well, sometimes I didn't know to expect company and sometimes company had their own keys. Imagine this: It is early in the morning, I'm snug asleep in bed, and my alarm goes off to get up for class. I wake up, sit up, and open my eyes to see two strange men standing in my bedroom.

Turns out the maintenance guys had come to fix my sink. They'd knocked, and when no one answered (because I was deaf and couldn't hear anything), they'd let themselves in with their spare key. Apparently I am a very quiet sleeper because they were in my bedroom fixing my sink for twenty minutes, not realizing there was a person in the bed.

Believe it or not, this wasn't an isolated incident. It also happened with the monthly cleaning service my complex hired—twice. And then my RA let herself into the apartment to "check on me." She entered while I was cleaning knives in the sink. That last one could have been really messy if I was a jumpier person.

As a result of all these incidents, I started to feel unsafe living by myself and was very grateful when a new little blond roommate moved into the vacant room.

School

Despite my current predicament I still had a goal to finish my two majors in four years. I drove (yes, deaf people can drive) down to the disability resource center on campus and talked to them about my options. I didn't know sign language, so an interpreter would be useless to me. However, the center did have the option of hiring real-time court captioners. This way, I would have a real-time transcript of what was being said in my classes. I decided to give that a try.

My classes were different now. I had a captioner placed in each one of them, and trust me, having a woman with a strange keyboard between her knees with you everywhere you go gets you noticed. I would walk into each class, and the captioner would be all set up on a chair next to my desk.

They had captioning machines, which were positioned on stands between their legs, and they typed away as my professors and classmates talked. On a desk placed in front of mine sat a laptop that was connected to their captioning machine/keyboards so that, as they typed, I could read the words off the laptop in real time.

These women were amazing; some of them became my dear friends. They were excellent sources of information and even advocated for me when I needed them to—like when a professor chose to ignore the school policies and show videos in class that did not have captioning making them accessible for the deaf.

The captioners gave me access to the information in class, but they also were a very large, very obvious physical reminder to me and everyone around me that I was different and that I was "disabled." I felt just like I had when I'd first started wearing my hearing aids. I felt lesser than my peers.

Yet in some weird way, I also felt special. Having that help, having access to information in a way I never had before, and having a special saved seat in each of my classes made me feel good. It was almost like the accommodation the school was providing me was the universe saying, "You belong here. See, we made a space for you."

Even with the help, classes were harder for me—especially my business calculus class. Being deaf gave me one of two options when it came to learning calculus. The first was to watch what the professor was writing on the board. The second was to read what she was saying off the laptop in front of me. Because I couldn't hear, I couldn't do both at the same time anymore.

The problem was that, without the explanation she was verbally giving, I couldn't understand the relationship between the numbers and progression she was writing on the board. And without the writing on the board, I couldn't visualize what she was explaining with her words.

I very quickly started to fall behind in class. I started going to the professor's office hours, but there weren't enough of those to keep me on track for the entire quarter. I joined a club called ARCHES, which provided me with a calculus tutor twice a week. This helped a lot, but I was still struggling in class.

On weekends, my little brother would drive home from USC, where he was now studying electrical engineering, and go over my homework assignments with me and answer any questions I had. Sometimes, having a superintelligent, overachieving brother comes in handy.

Yet even with all this effort and help, I still think I only managed to finish the class with a C+. Not being near the top of my class was new territory for me. Putting this much effort into something and feeling like I was still failing wasn't.

I did okay in the rest of my classes. I used to be an auditory learner. When I heard something, I remembered it. I loved listening to lectures. There was definitely a transition period where I was getting used to working with the captioner. I had to teach myself to read as fast as my captioners could type and my professors could talk. I also had to train my brain to absorb more information when I read it off the laptop in front of me in class.

Having captioners in my classes also came with its fair share of interesting moments—like the time one of my marketing teachers did a lecture on PepsiCo, and the captioner's machine auto corrected the word *Pepsi* to *penis* for an entire hour lecture. You try not laughing during that; it is hard.

Or the time, I had a professor with such a thick accent that every student sitting near me moved his or her desk closer in an attempt to read what the professor was saying off my captioning laptop because they couldn't understand a word of it on their own.

Baby steps

I had this one night class that year that let out around 9:00 p.m. I would have to walk in the dark across campus and then across the road to my apartment. Although campus was generally safe, I never felt safe crossing the street outside of campus alone at night back to my apartment complex.

When I was a junior, I used to call my mom when I got out of late classes and talk to her on the phone as I walked back to the parking structure to make myself feel safe. I still remember my last phone call like yesterday. I had called my mother as I was walking away from class, and I started rambling about all the events of my day.

I then stopped and waited for her reply; it didn't come. All I heard was some faint mumbling on the other line. The phone's volume was set to max. My heart sank as I told her, "Mom, I love you. I know you are talking, but I can't hear you anymore." Those words still kind of haunt me whenever I watch her take a business call, feeling a little envious that I can't simply pick up a phone and call her whenever I want to anymore.

Now, even though I could no longer hear her voice, our tradition of late-night phone calls while I walked home from class continued. It was just very one-sided. I would ramble on and on about my day. I would ask her questions, and she would text me her responses to the questions after we hung up. It wasn't perfect communication, but it was communication. Thank God for texting.

Mourning

The fact that I did my best to hide my hearing loss and ignore it as a child doesn't mean that was the best or easiest way to handle the situation. In the long run, it was actually the hardest, most painful way I could have reacted. Hearing loss isn't something one just overcomes and puts behind them.

What I didn't realize at the time was that, with all of this moving out and throwing myself into schoolwork, I was just keeping myself busy, trying to keep myself in denial, because I had lost something precious. A part of me had actually physically died, and I was delaying my mourning of this piece of me.

The best way I can try to describe it is as if you lose a sibling or a best friend. By losing your hearing, you lose a constant companion, a protector who warns you of danger, a link to the outside world who holds your hand through all social interaction, your concert buddy, your confidence. And in my case, I lost a little of my mind.

My brain didn't know how to handle the change from being a hearing person to becoming a deaf person. My brain was in denial. I looked at the world around me, and I saw all the amazing sounds happening, yet I physically could hear nothing. My brain couldn't process this, so it started guessing, trying to fill in blanks, making me feel like I was hearing things when I wasn't.

For example, every single day, to this day, when I get in the shower, my brain makes me "hear" the sound of running water. It even differentiates between the sounds of water showering down on an empty tub versus the water hitting my body. This sound is like a ghost; it is a past memory that I will never actually experience again, yet it stays with me even after my physical ability to perceive it has long gone.

I used to play this game in college—"the Listening Game" I called it. I would sit on a bench in the middle of campus, and I would watch students walk by and imagine all of the sounds they were making. The sound of a basic girl's Uggs crunching through the gravel, the sound of that rude kid on a bike swerving through the pedestrians on the sidewalk, his wheels spinning with a whirring sound. The clicking made as a professor on the adjacent bench unlatches his briefcase.

Every day, I would sit, watch, and imagine—no, I'd remember—all the different sounds this world makes. The shuffling of papers, the random cough in the back of the room, the clicking of a pen, my heartbeat.

I was so afraid that, if I stopped making myself remember these things every single day, I would forget them, that I would lose them. No matter how much I imagined and no matter how many dreams I had in which I could miraculously hear again, nothing changed. I was still deaf. A part of me was still physically dead, and that was never going to change. I am sure this wasn't exactly healthy, but the memories of sound were all I had left.

I remember going to the doctors after I'd lost the last of my functional hearing and asking them *why*? They still couldn't give me a straight answer. They gave me a bunch of possible scenarios, but all they could say for sure was, "You probably have nerve damage."

An average of two times a year since I was four years old, my mother would drive me to these doctors' offices. They would poke, prod, and test me. Then they would lock me away in the little padded room with the five-inch reinforced steel door and one large window so they could all stare at me like a zoo animal during my tests.

Then they would place the heavy headphones on my little ears, place a button in my hand, and tell me, "Press it when you hear the beep." Two times a year for eighteen years, I would sit in that room as they made me repeat the words *airplane* ... *hot dog* ... *ice cream* ... over and over and over again, testing my word recognition.

Yet in eighteen years, they could not tell me why I was losing my hearing. They could not give me a cause. They could not tell me if it would stabilize. They just kept locking me away in the room and "monitoring my progress." So now I sat on a bench at twenty-two years old imagining sounds, delaying my mourning, and lacking closure.

"Hearing Impaired"

I found myself feeling very alone and isolated at this point in my life. It is hard to go from being a social butterfly to becoming someone who is fearful and anxious during everyday social interactions. It is hard to retrain yourself to do everyday activities with a missing sense.

It is hard to hold a conversation without being able to hear what your partner is saying. When I didn't understand a person or when I had already had someone repeat him or herself a few times, I noticed that I started feeling guilty and like I owed the person some sort of explanation for using so much more of their time.

I started testing out words to help people understand that I couldn't hear them. *Hearing impaired* felt too negative to me, so that phrase was discarded. *Hard of hearing* made it seem like I could still hear something and that my hearing loss wasn't that bad, so it didn't work.

Finally, *deaf* felt too "disabled" to me. I still associated it with that negative stereotype, and I didn't want myself seen that way. Deciding what to call myself was a lot harder than one might assume.

I was starting to do well again in my classes, thanks to the accommodations the school was providing me. Even though my speech was getting stronger every day, I knew I needed to find a new way to communicate. I also knew that I needed to adjust and figure out a better way to connect with this world around me. I still felt just as lost, alone, and different as I had when I was as a kid. I lacked an identity. So I went searching for it.

I went down to the disability resource center on campus and asked if there were any other people like me, people who couldn't hear, on campus. I learned that there were. They met once a month to hang out and show each other some support. I got the group's contact information and arranged to join their next meeting.

I was so nervous! I wanted so badly to fit in anywhere, to be accepted and understood by anyone. I practiced my ABCs in sign language (thank you, high school sign language class) and a few random signs I could remember and went to meet them. Including me, there were five of us total.

On a campus with tens of thousands of students, there were only five students with varying levels of hearing loss. Two of them used spoken language and sign language to communicate, and two of them were sign language users only. I couldn't keep up with their signing.

I felt ashamed that I had never become fluent. I felt ashamed that I knew nothing about deaf culture or day-to-day things, like how deaf people made phone calls or went to the movies. I felt ignorant, intimidated, and scared. I tried to stick with it. I went to a few more gatherings, but I didn't feel comfortable in that environment.

When I confided this information to my mother, she decided to try to help me out by hiring a private sign language tutor to come to the house and teach my entire family sign language at the same time. She figured that, if I got a better handle on the language, I would feel more comfortable with the new group of friends.

Everyone showed up for the first lesson—my aunts, uncles, cousins, grandmother, brother, and parents were all there. My grandmother quit about twenty minutes into the first lesson. The second lesson, a few people were "busy." The third lesson, more family members were "too busy." Before I knew it, they had all dropped out one by one, except my mother.

She seemed always to be there for me. I felt like I wasn't important enough to my other family members for them to sacrifice one hour of their time a week to be able to simply learn how to communicate with me. I was angry, disappointed, and hurt. Was it my fault?

Had I adapted too well and talked too well all these years so that they couldn't even see how much I was struggling, how much I needed this? Had I made their lives too easy when I'd decided that hearing loss was my burden to bear? I tortured myself with these questions each night before crying myself to sleep.

The sign language tutor was offered another job, and after just a few months, it was just my mother and I showing up to learn. So my mother reluctantly canceled the lessons. I went back to bottling up my feelings and not showing them to my family members.

I tried to continue hanging out with the deaf group on campus, but I just wasn't ready to accept myself as a deaf person. I still hadn't gone through the mourning stages. I hadn't gotten to the acceptance stage yet. I continued to live my life the hard way, trying to fit in with hearing people and do everything like a hearing person does, even when I knew I simply couldn't hear.

Socially

College is a time of experimentation. While most college students are experimenting with alcohol and interpersonal relationships, I spent my time experimenting with new ways to tell people I couldn't hear without having them literally run away from me. Seriously, you would have thought I had told them that I had the plague or something. Whether it was in class, at a party, or on a date, my deafness seemed to scare people away.

There was an odd twist to being deaf. I was all of a sudden being praised for just having the courage to get out of bed in the morning. Every little thing I did people called "inspirational"—whether I had finished a homework assignment, like everyone else, or simply remembered to bring a pen to class with me.

My peers couldn't imagine a life without sound, so they put me on this weird pedestal where they could admire me but also keep me separate from them. For example, most of my classmates would smile and give me a friendly wave as if we were close friends every day before class, but no one would sit in the desks directly next to mine. When it came time to work on a group project, no one wanted me in his or her group.

I had spent nearly my entire life feeling different, but this was the first time in my life people were actually treating me in this manner.

I learned quickly that people have an interesting way of reacting to meeting a person with hearing loss for the first time. The encounter usually begins with questions like, "How do you talk?" "Can you drive?" "How do you watch movies?" The list goes on and on. To each of these questions, I started to develop a witty, sometimes sarcastic response.

This was usually around the lines of, "Well just because my ears stopped working doesn't mean my vocal chords did," or, "Yes I can drive. Why would I need my ears for that?"

However, at this point in my life, some people or organizations were having some bizarre responses to my disability. It wasn't just individuals; companies, organizations, and groups of people began revealing their ignorance about deafness to me on a more frequent basis.

For example, when I purchased airline tickets and I clicked the box during the purchasing process to ask for special assistance due to my disability. I was flying to meet my cousins in Hawaii. I entered into the computer a request for assistance with my hearing disability, thinking this meant that the attendants would turn captions on for the safety video, maybe tell me when my group was boarding, or maybe go the extra mile and turn captions on for the in-flight entertainment. I didn't think these were ridiculously high expectations.

Yet, none of that happened. They did, however, have a lovely wheelchair—with my name literally written on it in big black bold letters, "AMANDA MCDONOUGH"—waiting for me at the plane's door when I landed in Hawaii (and again back in LAX). Well, that was all fine and dandy, but my legs work. My ears don't. It was awkward.

Sadly, years later, this airline problem still hasn't been addressed. Most airlines still don't caption their in-flight entertainment, and I still, more often than not, have wheelchairs awaiting me upon arrival at my destinations.

Another shocker for me came at a local movie theater. After a couple years of avoiding seeing films while they were in theaters and waiting for them to come out on DVD or Redbox, I finally discovered that one of our local movie theaters offered closed captioning machines for the deaf to watch movies too.

I was so excited to finally be able to see films with everyone else! When I approached the guest assistance desk and asked for a captioning machine for the deaf, the attendant disappeared under the desk, only to pop back up holding a big book of braille.

He offered the book to me and I had to politely explain that I don't read braille and that I was actually looking for a machine that displayed the movie lines in English. His supervisor was able to help me explain the concept of a captioning device to his employee, and I was eventually handed one to use to enjoy the film I had selected. I was definitely surprised, though, to learn how much this young man didn't know about people with hearing loss.

Hanging out with my friends from high school started to also become frustrating. I had to ask them again and again to turn on the captioning when we watched movies or if I could sit in a seat with a clearer view of the TV. They interpreted these requests as me being a diva.

Yet, for me, these were simply changes I needed to function. I could no longer participate in their random bursting-into-song moments. Even the games we usually played like Apples to Apples or Disney DVD trivia (which didn't come with a captioning option) were impossible for me to participate in.

Before I knew it, my friends were inviting me out less and less, even though they were hanging out together more and more. When I confronted them about it, my concern was shrugged off.

I knew I was the one who was changing; I blamed myself, thinking that maybe I had complained too much or asked for too much special treatment. Maybe I had pushed them away. I felt the same way I had in junior high school—abandoned, unworthy, and unwanted.

It wasn't any better when it came to dating and meeting guys. For example, once I went to College Night at the Getty Museum with a group from a club I was involved in called ARCHES. We were hanging out, looking at art, watching live music, and generally enjoying the festivities when a college guy walked up to me and my two friends and started a conversation.

He seemed particularly interested in my answer to his questions. It turns out he was hitting on me (a concept I was not too familiar with in college and which flies right over my head to this day). After a short enjoyable banter, the conversation ended, and my two friends and I turned to walk away.

Apparently he chased after us calling my name (which of course I didn't hear). When he caught up and tapped my shoulder, I turned around. He looked angry and said, "What? Are you ignoring me now?"

My friend explained that I was deaf and simply couldn't hear him calling my name.

His response was a look of shock, accompanied by the phrase. "How do you function?"

In my head, I responded, "My heart still beats, my lungs still breathe, and my brain still works—unlike yours." But aloud I simply said, "Quite well, thanks" and walked away, wishing I had been quicker on my feet with a witty response.

I began limiting my social interaction and day-to-day activities even more. I only shopped at stores I had previously shopped at, only ate at restaurants where I knew the menu like the back of my hand, and (when possible) I only banked with a machine, not a person.

I scripted my orders at coffee shops so that no possible follow-up questions that could be asked. I scripted all of my day-to-day interactions as much as possible to avoid as much communication as possible. When a stranger felt chatty, I simply nodded and smiled and agreed with whatever he or she was saying. Even though 90 percent of the time I had no idea what the person was saying, I got very good at reacting appropriately to body language. I laughed when people laughed, smiled when they smiled, and shook my head in disapproval when they did. Questions always threw me off, though.

When someone asked me a question on the topic of the conversation I had been a part of for the last fifteen minutes, I looked like an idiot fumbling for the most generic answers possible, trying to change the subject, or trying to divert attention away from myself by asking the person a question about his or her question.

Yes, it was that confusing. People started calling me a "great listener." They misinterpreted my inability to contribute to the conversation and eagerness to keep them talking so I didn't have to as me being genuinely interested in them and what they had to say. Honestly, I would have killed to know what they were saying, but that wasn't my motivation for sitting there quietly and attentively, looking them straight in the eyes as they went on and on about a topic.

Almost every aspect of my life was falling apart. My friends were MIA, doing basic adult things had become unbearably stressful, and I felt like I could no longer function at a basic human level. I knew I was a strong, intelligent young woman, but every interaction with another human being left me feeling like an incompetent idiot.

I grew up in fear of my hearing loss turning me into this isolated, uneducated being who couldn't communicate or socialize. I felt like my nightmare was becoming a reality. I had traded in a fun, social job at Disneyland for an internship at my mom's company that didn't require me to interact with others. My classes began feeling impossible, and my grades began reflecting that.

I worked ten times harder than any other college student I had ever met. While my peers were going to parties, raves, clubs, or concerts, I was hiding in my room studying.

The parties and the crowded scenes are something I could do without. Loud, dark, noisy, and distracting environments began to make it nearly impossible for me to communicate. There were times I did go to a bar or a club with some of my friends, and a guy would come up to me and try to talk to me.

I would gesture that I didn't understand him and his first reaction would always be to yell directly in my ear (yeah ...seriously). I still remember the first time this happened to me. I pointed to my ear and said, "Sorry, I can't hear." The guy's reaction was to nod in agreement and say, "Yeah this music is crazy loud. I can't hear either."

That poor clueless guy had no idea that I was serious. He just shrugged it all off and kept trying to get my number. At least I think that is what he was asking for. He could have been asking me my opinions on post-9/11 air travel for all I know. What I do know is that I felt embarrassed and uncomfortable every time anyone would try to talk to me in these environments.

I spent those nights guessing at what people were saying or asking, faking my reaction to stories based on body language and social cues, and avoiding anyone with an accent or thick facial hair. It was just easier to stay away from bars, clubs, raves, or concerts and hang out in intimate, small groups or gatherings instead. At least that is what I told myself so that I didn't feel like I was being left out of a critical youthful experience.

Surprisingly, I still managed to have a few short relationships. College guys tend to have short attention spans and be pretty flakey, so I didn't have high expectations for any of the guys I dated in college. However, these guys were great for figuring out how my deafness factored into a relationship with another human being and for a few healthy heartbreaks.

My roommates affectionately nicknamed a few of them: "The Coward" changed his relationship status on Facebook to "single" before sending me a breakup text (yes, he broke up with me in a text). "The Jerk" slept with his best friend's crush while the three of them were in Las Vegas and then came home to drop me like a sack of potatoes. "The Sweetheart" was the nicest guy alive but was afraid to ever make a move. "The Fake Friend" had a tendency to lead me on and then make me feel crazy for thinking he cared about me as more than a friend.

My luck when it came to boys/men didn't improve, but at least I hadn't become a total pariah. I made a few executive decisions for myself during this period in my life. I would never rely on my partner for communication; I would never date another frat guy type; and I would let people get to know me first, before telling them that I couldn't hear.

You see, if I led with the "deaf thing," guys wouldn't even give me a chance. But if I started the date with my dates getting to know me and slipped the "deaf thing" in casually at the end or maybe on the second or third date, then guys were more likely to not think it was such a big deal and allow themselves to get to know me for me.

My inability to hear always seemed to become a factor that bothered the guys I was dating, though. Having to remember to look at me when they talked apparently was one of the most frustrating things in the world for some guys. I mean I was the one doing the hard work by lipreading, but just the fact that I couldn't understand them if I wasn't looking at them was enough to frustrate some guys to no end.

Logically, I knew a guy who couldn't handle this wasn't the right guy for me. After all, my hearing wasn't magically going to come back. In the moment, however, it still hurt. And each new relationship that I had left behind was a little more damaging to my self-esteem.

10

I THINK I CAN:
DIDN'T GIVE UP ON MY DREAMS

While there were admittedly a lot of things in my life that weren't perfect and I had a lot of adjusting to do, I never lost hope that I would make it through this tough transition period in my life.

I really just focused on taking everything day by day, class by class, and conversation by conversation. When it came to the future, I didn't really have a plan. It was hard for me to picture my future. All I knew is that I had to get through today before I could figure out tomorrow.

Got back into acting

One morning, I woke up; checked my Facebook, per my normal morning ritual; and realized I had a Facebook message from a guy I had known back at Disneyland. They called him Katz. I was surprised to receive his message; I was even more surprised to read its contents.

He basically explained that he had friends who owned a production company that produced murder mystery dinner shows. Apparently, their lead actress had dropped out on them at the last possible moment.

They only had about two weeks until their first performance, and they needed to replace her. He remembered people saying good things about my work as an actress and asked if I would be interested in taking the part on such short notice.

I remember thinking to myself, *Well, that would have been a fun thing to do if I could still hear.* I missed theater, I missed acting, and I missed who I was onstage. Feeling defeated, I went to visit my grandmother and dramatically dropped myself onto her bed.

I wished I could do it, take the role, but I was deaf. How was I supposed to hear the other lines? How was I supposed to get my cues? How was I supposed to interact with an audience? *They wouldn't want a girl who can't hear as the lead in their play anyways,* I convinced myself.

My grandmother asked why I was making an ugly face, and I explained the situation to her.

She simply said, "Do it."

I countered with, "But how? I can't hear."

To this, she responded, "You are smart and talented, and you have never let your hearing stop you before. Why would you start now? Besides, you will regret it for the rest of your life if you don't try."

This conversation continued for a few more minutes until she convinced me that I could do it. I messaged Katz back and told him I was in!

He forwarded me the script. It was over fifty pages long, and when he'd said I would be taking over for the "lead girl," he had literally meant lead. I had more than 50 percent of the lines in the entire play!

I printed out the script and got to highlighting and memorizing. The first rehearsal date was set, and I was beyond nervous. I drove out to Riverside, hoping I could fool all these people into thinking I could hear them. I didn't want them to know I couldn't hear. I didn't want them to think I was incapable.

I showed up to that first rehearsal with almost all of my lines memorized, as well as the lines of the other characters. I had timed out scenes in my head so I knew basically how long it was between my lines. I was as prepared as I could be in just two days.

I could tell they were nervous too. They were paid performers who were taking a huge risk hiring a girl they had never worked with, let alone heard of. I was determined to pull my weight. Katz introduced me to the owners of the company, Cash and Carrie.

They were a wonderful couple who also performed in their shows and looked younger than their years. They introduced me to the rest of the cast—great performers and people who I would become good friends with. We started rehearsal, and they seemed impressed that I was so prepared.

I did my best to keep up but every scene had three or more characters in it, which made it incredibly difficult to follow who was talking. Also, this company was made up of skilled ad-libbers, so after months of rehearsals, their lines had evolved into something that maintained the plot but didn't necessarily follow the script in a word-for-word manner.

Nothing I ever did could be easy, right? Luckily for me, I found the pattern within the first few runs of the scenes. The actors were very focused on physical comedy, so I didn't have to obsess over the words so much. Their bodies also told the story. I started picking up my cues from the choreography and blocking.

When I wasn't facing a character, I learned to feel the vibrations of the actor's voice or movements, which would alert me to when a line started and stopped or when a character entered the scene. Now, I wasn't perfect, but I did manage to fool the company into believing I could hear the other actors and myself.

I delivered my lines as written and ad-libbed when necessary, and the show started flowing together quite smoothly. In a short two weeks, we were ready to perform our first show at a country club. I was nervous. I read over my lines again and again backstage. I knew where I was weak and kept yellow sticky tabs in the pages I needed to look over again between scenes, but it was a blast! The energy was great, the show flowed nicely, and the audience enjoyed it.

Before the show and during intermission, we went from table to table interacting in character with the audience. We were supposed to answer questions and give small clues. I had scripted my "performance" at the tables in a way that would require the least amount of interaction and made my answers so generic that, no matter what someone asked, I technically answered the question. My family even purchased a table to come see my first performance in many years.

When it was over, I felt proud of myself. I felt invincible. I had worked so hard for this moment, and it felt good. We had a few more performances at this beautiful old-fashioned theater in Riverside called The Fox. Its staircases and red velvet curtains were romantic to me. It had beautiful old Hollywood-style embellishments that made me fall in love. I loved the theater, and I loved performing. It felt good to be back.

Cash and Carrie must have loved my performance because they asked me to come back and be in their next show. I didn't even have to audition! The catch? I simply had to show them I could do a French accent. Me, the deaf girl who couldn't even hear my natural Californian accent, was supposed to do a French one!

Growing up, I had been obsessed with accents. I'd walked around for days pretending I was British or Russian. I'd loved making up strange voices for new characters and bringing them to life. If I had possessed the ability to hear my own voice at this point, I would not have broken a sweat. I would have simply gone home and learned a French accent. Again, I doubted my abilities, but I took on the challenge headfirst.

I went home to my apartment and first apologized to my roommate for the amount of random sounds that would probably be coming out of my room that night. Then I sat down at my desk, went to YouTube and started searching for videos of French people speaking English.

I found this one vlog that was interesting, and I started mimicking the way the young French girl moved her lips, but I didn't feel like the sound I was producing was quite right. I searched for videos of vocal coaches teaching different dialects and watched hours of videos on vocal placement and how different vowels are pronounced in different languages.

Then I practiced using the muscle memory I had built up in childhood and perfected in junior high and high school choir classes. Eventually, I was able to produce an understandable French accent. Granted, it was a bit cheesy, but so was the character I was working to portray, so it worked!

I started learning that doubting myself was simply a waste of time. I decided that I would retire the word *can't* again. I may have been deaf, but I could still accomplish anything I put my mind to.

Amanda stands holding the hands of her cast mates at the end of a dress rehearsal for a C&C Production play.

Music

Not long after my second play with C&C Productions, on a random warm day, my parents decided to drag me to an outdoor church music festival. I was in a sour mood that afternoon for no particular reason, but my dad ushered me into the crowd beneath a makeshift wooden stage with hand-me-down church speakers blasting.

On the stage was a group of middle-aged men who were living out their rock star dreams playing oldies. I could see in my dad's eyes he wanted me to react and enjoy the music like we used to when I was a kid—like when he and I would have daddy-daughter days at Disneyland watching the bands at Tomorrowland Terrace.

So I sucked up some of the bitterness I was radiating, put on a fake smile, and started swaying along with the crowd. The first song played and then a second. I could feel the bass and the drums, but the songs were lost on me. I kind of zoned out for a little bit as I swayed to the visual rhythm of the crowd surrounding me, guessing at the tone and beat of the songs.

I was lost in my own mind for a few minutes and then was jerked out of my thoughts abruptly by a moment of recognition. I recognized the song! I realized that my body had started swaying to the beat on its own. I wasn't guessing. I could actually feel the notes, feel the music against my skin. I looked up at my dad with tears pouring from my eyes as my lips formed the words "Sweet Home Alabama" exactly in time with the music.

My father looked shocked as I continued to yell the lyrics along with the band and the crowd at the top of my lungs. I had never felt anything like it. All the years I had listened to music, I was "deaf" to the actual feeling of music. For the first time in my life, I realized music is just vibrations floating through the air.

People who can hear interpret those vibrations through their eardrums. My whole body had woken up, stepped up, and volunteered my sense of touch as my new way of feeling music since my ears were out of commission. Each note was absorbed by my body in a way that was almost euphoric. My dad didn't question what had just happened in that old field behind a church. He simply accepted that his daughter would never cease to surprise him and let it be.

That night when we returned home, my dad went rummaging through the closet in his recording studio at home and found that big yellow bag full of all my old CDs. He walked into my room; handed me the bag; and said, "Don't give up."

So I shut the door and started playing the CDs one by one, with my hand against the boom box trying to decipher each individual vibration it was gifting me. I sat there alone trying to find my way back to music.

Graduated from College

I had done it! In four years, I had managed to finish the curriculum for both of my majors! I was officially set to graduate with a bachelor of science in business administration, double majoring in international business and marketing management, with an emphasis in entertainment marketing from California Polytechnic University, Pomona, with a 3.15 GPA! After so many setbacks, after so many struggles, it was finally going to be a reality!

Graduation day was hot, in the nineties. I had splurged on a new dress and these tall heels for the ceremony. All I could think of as I attempted to walk gracefully in them was, *Don't trip. Don't you dare trip.* My mom had made signs that spelled out my name and took up nearly an entire row of the outdoor venue. I had arranged for a captioner so that I didn't miss the announcer saying my name or any of the speeches.

*Amanda's family members hold up letters
spelling out her name at her college graduation.*

I sat near the stage with my captioner eagerly awaiting my turn. Then I saw the volunteer beckon me to stand in the line near the bottom of the stage with my peers to await my name. A he stood with me, his hand on my shoulder holding me in place. Then I felt a tap on my back, indicating to me that it was my turn to walk up on that stage and be handed my diploma.

It was different than my high school graduation. It was strange not being able to hear my name called, but as soon as I got up on that stage and looked out upon that crowd, with a triumphant smile on my face, I knew in my heart that my family was out there screaming and cheering louder than any other family possibly could.

I felt pride in myself and this gigantic accomplishment. I could have given up when I went deaf. I could have retreated within myself, and no one would have blamed me or judged me for it. Yet I didn't. I chose the harder path. I chose to stick with my goals. I chose to finish my education no matter what. And in that moment, on that stage, I knew I was now a stronger person for it.

Joe, Andrew, Amanda, and Julie McDonough
celebrate Amanda's college graduation.

Part 2

FINDING MY VOICE

I think I always knew deep down that I would become deaf. I may have fought it, denied it, and hid it for a good portion of my life, but it has always been a part of who I am. Once I was finally able to accept that part of me, my life's purpose became clear.

—Amanda McDonough

11

HALF WOMAN-HALF MACHINE: COCHLEAR IMPLANT SURGERY

Even though I had achieved a lot since losing my hearing, the pain, humiliation, and anxiety I went through every day in all social interactions started to take their toll on me. I started to wonder what I would do now that I had graduated from college. Where would I work? How would I communicate? Would I ever make new friends? Would people ever accept me with my hearing loss?

Every single second of my day felt like a struggle. Every time I couldn't understand a person or had someone repeat him or herself, I felt like a failure. I was beating myself up and mentally punishing myself for not being able to move through this world as easily as my hearing peers. I kept working my ass off to be better, smarter, or faster, just so that I could barely keep up, and it was wearing me down.

Learning about Cochlear Implants

I decided to make an appointment with a new specialist to see if anything could be done about my hearing. The specialist introduced me to the idea of this surgery called cochlear implant surgery. However, the thought of letting someone cut open my head and burn out my cochlear hair cells didn't really appeal to me at the time, no matter how desperate I was.

My new doctor suggested tests and extremely high dosages of

steroids to see if we could restimulate my dead nerves. The steroids made me gain roughly thirty pounds in only twenty-eight days; I had moon face, hair growth, mood swings, and hormonal issues—the works.

The tests proved that my hearing loss was not genetic but couldn't produce a definitive cause. It was not a glamorous process, but I was desperate to get some of my hearing back so I could utilize hearing aids again. And I needed answers.

Just like when I was a kid, I prayed, not for all of my hearing to return but just enough to function. Yet it seems God had a different plan for me because the steroid treatments yielded no change in my hearing.

Even though I hadn't decided whether or not to have cochlear implant surgery, I did decide to get all the testing done to see if I was even a candidate for the surgery. While everyone else was throwing graduation parties, I was going through MRIs; hearing evaluations; blood tests; and, worst of all, a balance test.

If you can avoid ever having a balance test, avoid it. It is basically a legal form of Chinese water torture. I thought all I would have to do was walk on a balance beam. I had no idea I would be strapped to a board and have steaming hot and freezing cold water power sprayed into my ears, causing my brain and body to become disoriented. It felt like I was in one of those astronaut-training balls that flip you every which way till you puke. For the record, I didn't puke. Which I guess means I passed.

Wasn't an Easy Decision

At the end of all the tests, I found out that I was a candidate for surgery. However, one does not simply decide to have cochlear implant surgery, just as one does not simply walk into Mordor. It hadn't even been a year since my tonsillectomy, and now I was being faced with another possible surgery. This one, however, was much more terrifying to me. I simply wanted to stop feeling like every day was a struggle and to give myself every possible opportunity to be successful in this life.

I went back and forth with that decision for months. I knew the implant wouldn't give me back my natural hearing; nothing could. And if I chose to have the surgery, the surgeons would be burning out the cochlear hair cells in my ear, meaning I would never be able to hear naturally through that ear ever again.

I was still secretly holding out hope for a biological solution to hearing loss in the future; this felt like a lot to possibly sacrifice. I figured that, if I chose to have the surgery, I would compromise by only having one ear implanted and saving the natural makeup of the other to see if medical advances could grant me any natural hearing in the future.

I had started interviewing for jobs near the end of my senior year of college, and no one would hire me. It was at that time that I started seriously considering the surgery. I wanted so desperately to be independent and successful and to reconnect with the world I had been cut off from for so long. The surgery started to feel like the only way this could happen.

I would go into these job interviews, and the interviewer would be talking down into a computer or holding up my résumé, covering his or her lips while asking me questions so I couldn't lip-read. I would end up looking like a complete idiot in every job interview.

Jobs were already scarce, the economy sucked, and most of my friends who had graduated before me were underemployed. Now I had to compete for those scarce jobs against my peers with the same qualifications as me but who could also hear. I was screwed.

I didn't get a single job offer by the time graduation rolled around, and I was starting to think I would be working for my mom's company forever. I couldn't bear the thought of relying on anyone but myself, of not being independent, and of being unemployed!

One day, I drove back to my mom's house, walked through the door with a determined gait, and walked up to my mom. "I am getting it," I said. "That's it. End of discussion." Then I left. That was that.

Soon after graduation, I was scheduled for my cochlear implant surgery. It was a scary and exciting time for me. I had this weird, illogical idea stuck in my head that I had to do everything I loved one last time before the surgery—as if having this machine in my head would change who I was or how I experienced life.

I basically made a bucket list. I traveled, went to nearly every theme park in California, ate at all my favorite restaurants (like BJ's Pizza and Benihana), and spent lots of time with the people I loved. It felt like it was the end of something. Or was it the beginning? I had no idea.

I had done my research. I knew I wasn't going to have perfect hearing after the surgery, and what I would have wouldn't be natural hearing. I knew it was an outpatient surgery and that there was healing time between the implantation and receiving my external processor; therefore, there would be a gap in time between the surgery and me hearing for the first time.

I even was required to sign a piece of paper that stated that I understood that I would never understand or enjoy music the same again. I knew not to expect miracles going into this experience. But I had a few fantasies, no dreams, for my future that required me to be able to hear.

I wanted to be able to use a phone again so that I could have my independence back. I wanted to be able to hear my future husband say, "I do," on my wedding day. And lastly, I wanted to be able to hear the first cries of my future children as they announced their arrival to the world.

These were the moments I prayed for, but they were not guaranteed even with the surgery.

The Reporter

Brian Calvert was the brother of the owners of C&C Productions, the production company that I had worked with on the mystery dinner shows through college. He and I met at one of the wrap parties for a show. He was a bit older than me, but I remember having a kid-type crush on him when we first met.

I really liked the way his mind worked, not to mention how amazing his job was. He was well traveled, well spoken, and had an air of worldliness about him. For his job, he traveled all over the world documenting the life stories of amazing people.

What I didn't know when I met him was that he already had heard all about me from his sister, Carrie. At the cast party, we all sat in a circle, and everyone from the theater company recounted their personal stories of how they had no idea I was deaf until I finally told them halfway through rehearsals for the second show.

Everyone told his or her own funny "I should have known when ..." stories about me not reacting to something or ignoring someone for days. It was a little embarrassing, but we all laughed. It was a great wrap party.

Later, Brian pulled me to the side and asked if I would be willing to sit down with him and tell him my story for a radio broadcast show. I was surprised. I honestly didn't think I was anything special. I didn't see any inspiration in my life story. I was ashamed of it, ashamed of my hearing loss. I saw only struggle. It was so surprising to me that anyone could take what I had been through and see bravery in it.

I eventually agreed to allow him to interview me for a story. I was so nervous! I had never told my story before. I had literally kept my hearing loss a complete secret for eighteen years of my life. I never spoke about it. I never talked of my struggles. I never recounted stories of my childhood that had anything to do with my ears or sound. I didn't know how to tell my story, where to start, what was interesting, or what was relevant.

Most people have a handful of go-to stories from their childhood, stories they have told so many times that they have found the perfect formula of how to tell it to get the maximum reaction from their audience. I didn't have those. The memories of losing my hearing were so painful that my mind had actually blocked many of them out. There is so much of my childhood that my parents must remind me of because, for me, it was simply something I did not want to remember. Even now, as an adult, I find my brain still files away hearing-loss related memories into a folder that requires a painful amount of digging to uncover. This honestly has made writing this book almost impossible.

No one had actually ever heard any of my stories other than my mother and a few very close friends. Then Brian came around with his sound-recording equipment and big fluffy microphone. My mom worried for me. I didn't know how to tell my story.

I wanted to tell it in a way that didn't come off as complaining but also in a way that showed I was human, flawed, and relatable. At first, I thought we would simply sit at my kitchen table for an hour, and I would tell him a story about a girl who grew up wearing hearing aids. But this story became more than that because Brian saw that there was more to me.

Radio broadcast reporter Brian
Calvert interviews Amanda.

We spent countless hours sitting in my home, in a car, and on the park bench where I used to run away from my problems. I told him the truth; I became so comfortable talking with him that it was therapeutic. Sometimes I would even forget he was recording. When I had a bad day, I wanted to tell him about it.

We became great friends. One day, we took a walk in the park and just talked about art, music, literature, politics, and philosophy. It was nice to watch him talk for a change, instead of just sitting there with his intent eyes and ears absorbing everything I said.

I remember one specific afternoon. My uncle and aunts were over at my house. As usual, everyone was laughing and smiling and connecting.

I couldn't make out the conversations. Everyone was talking over each other. There were sounds coming from every direction.

I was sitting there with a blank expression. I sat in silence, separated from everyone I know and love. I was in a crowded room but felt completely alone. Normally, I would hold in the pain I was feeling, but this particular night was the breaking point for me. I couldn't handle the loneliness. My eyes began to water.

I couldn't stop the tears, but I couldn't bear the thought of my family seeing me cry. To me, making them feel upset or uncomfortable was the greatest sin I could commit. I pushed back my chair and sprinted out the front door. I ran for two miles before I caught my breath. Tears were streaming down my face, and my whole body was shaking uncontrollably.

I couldn't stop crying. I cried as if I hadn't cried in years. I am embarrassed to admit that I felt sorry for myself. The feeling of loneliness and longing stung in my chest. It burned and ached and stabbed. It was a sensation that I had carried with me every day for years, but on this night, it blazed to life with a fury that made me wish I could end it all.

I knew true loneliness in this moment. No one came after me. The sun set, and I sat in the dark alone until the tears finally stopped. I then walked myself home. Everyone was still there, sitting around drinking coffee. I walked in, and they looked up. No one said anything, or if they did I obviously couldn't hear it.

I walked straight into my room. I didn't feel like I belonged there anymore. I didn't feel like I belonged to that happy, loving family surrounding the table. I was the outcast. I went in my room and closed the door. I wasn't bothered. I took out the recording device Brian had given me from the drawer beside my bed and began recounting the night's experience into the little fuzzy microphone.

I talked to him even though he was not there, and I felt better, not so alone. I knew my family would never understand me, not really. Going deaf is such a rare human experience, one that can only be understood by going through it oneself.

I love my family, but even today I still feel like an outcast. I still find myself feeling alone in a room full of these happy, loud Italian Americans. I still hit that breaking point, though I have learned to deal with it better over time.

Surgery

On July 3, 2012, I went into the hospital with my mother, father, brother, Auntie Jayia, and Brian. I tried to be strong for them, but I was so scared. My surgery was scheduled for late morning, but there were two other patients the hospital moved before me and a small confrontation with the insurance company.

The insurance company had previously approved the surgery but then tried to get out of paying the bill at the last possible second. My dad dealt with the insurance issue.

Finally, many hours later, at about 3:00 p.m., the pre-op preparations began—hospital bracelets, IVs, and fluids; drawing blood and checking to make sure I hadn't eaten; heart rate monitors and vitals checking; last-minute meetings with the doctor and the anesthesiologists; and an ugly hospital gown to tie it all together.

My mother was with me through the whole process. She kept a smile on my face by telling me stories and teasing on me the whole time. My dad, brother, aunt, and Brian were confined to the waiting room during the pre-op preparations.

Then I was wheeled into the pre-op room. My mother was not allowed in there, but Brian had gotten special permission beforehand to accompany me and record my journey until they put me to sleep. I remember watching the nurses try to ask me questions through their sanitary masks.

I could see the outline of their lips moving under the fabric, and I remember thinking, *They know I can't hear them, right? I mean that's why I'm here for this surgery.*

Thank goodness for Brian. He had become a close friend the past few months while he had been documenting my story. He repeated the questions for me, so I could read his lips. They then shaved the right side of my head. Yes, you have me to thank for that side-shaved hairstyle fad that has been sweeping the country these last few years. Just kidding ... maybe.

I think that is the moment it hit me. I realized that, in a few more minutes, my doctor would be cutting through my scalp, burning out my cochlear hair cells, running wires through my head, shaving out a piece of my skull, and putting a piece of machinery inside of me. I had been working so hard to keep up this brave face for my family and friends that I hadn't actually had the opportunity to mentally prepare for what was about to happen to me.

I didn't have much time to dwell on this realization because they then cleaned my shaved head and wheeled me into the actual operating room. The last things I remember were the nurses putting a pillow under my knees and tucking me in with warm blankets and the anesthesiologist saying, "Count back from ten." To this, I responded, "It smells like mint," and immediately blacked out. That's when Brian was asked to step out of the operating room.

When I came to consciousness, I couldn't open my eyes or move my body. I remember feeling trapped and panicked. I don't know how long it was before I was able to open my eyes. When I finally did, I could just make out a blurry clock on a wall and some worried-looking nurses who appeared to be talking to me.

Obviously, I wasn't responding. I couldn't hear them. I also couldn't move to react to them. It took a while before I could part my lips, and they offered me water. At some point, I was rolled into the recovery room where family could visit me. Cochlear implant surgery is supposed to be a relatively easy outpatient surgery, but it took me longer than normal to regain use of my arms.

I couldn't breathe, and my throat was all scratched up from the breathing tube. I could barely swallow, and I kept choking and gagging. My dad had to take my younger brother and the reporter out of the room because I was in such bad shape. The nurse kept trying to get me to go to the bathroom so she could send me home, but I couldn't move my legs.

My Auntie Jayia was holding my hand, crying, while my mom tried to help me drink apple juice through a straw. Hours later, the two of them had to basically carry me to the bathroom so that I could pee and the nurse could officially release me. I still couldn't really walk on my own. The anesthesia and muscle relaxers still hadn't worn off quite yet.

My parents lifted me out of the wheelchair in front of the hospital and into our car. It was late, like 9:00 p.m. that night, and we finally were on our way home. I slept until the next day.

The days following were a blur of Vicodin and family visitors. I remember watching reruns of NCIS for days during recovery and trying to find ways to keep the hair I had left away from the healing incision. It was a time of silence but with hope for the first time in a long time.

You see, with cochlear implant surgery, the surgeons put the implant in your head, and then your head must heal before you receive the external processor (which contains the power source that makes the implant work and the microphone that picks up sound). The implant alone is useless.

I waited for the incision on my head to heal, ate lots of ice cream, and watched marathons of my favorite shows. There was some dizziness involved in my healing process. Sometimes, I felt like I was on a boat in the middle of a storm. Recovery was painful, but I was no stranger to pain, physical or emotional.

On the bright side, the Vicodin stupor I was in entertained my brother. Apparently, I walked around the house one day after surgery waving my arms in the air like a display air tube person at a used car dealership and saying, "Look everyone! My arms are like spaghetti!"

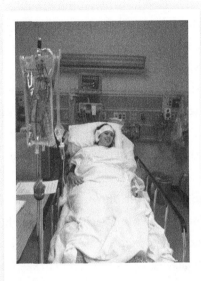

Amanda lays in a hospital bed after surgery with her head bandaged.

When my incision had healed, I returned to the ear specialists, and my doctor inspected it. I remember the incision area not looking pretty during healing; there were pus-filled bumps around the stitches, ingrown hairs, and a sore area around where the stitches had been. I couldn't sleep on the right side of my head (the side with the implant). My doctor assured me that I was healing as well as could be expected and signed me off as ready for my processor fitting.

Hearing for the First Time ... Again

This was the moment I had been waiting for—the moment the doctor would turn this piece of machinery in my head on, and I would hear again for the first time. I was excited and nervous.

Crammed into this small room was my audiologist, Brian, Andrew (my brother), my now ex-boyfriend, my mother, my father, and myself. My mother actually videotaped the whole thing. I still can't watch it without crying or wondering why I decided to wear that unflattering blue dress that day.

I still remember the odd sensation of the processor connecting to the implant for the first time. It is this weird magnetic pinch feeling. All that stood between the two pieces of technology was a thin layer of skin on my head. It felt heavy at first, but over time I have become accustomed to the weight.

There are two parts to the processor that is the external piece of equipment—the magnet, which attaches magnetically to the implant, and the battery pack/microphone, which looks like a hearing aid (only much larger, much heavier, and much harder to keep on my ear). These two pieces are connected by a wire that runs between them. It's a design that works but that I sincerely hope will be improved upon in the very near future.

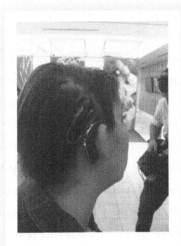

*A close-up of Amanda's cochlear
implant processor on her head.*

In this small room, my audiologist attached the processor to my head and also to her computer. The first sound I heard was a clear beep. It was the same kind of beep that I'd heard growing up in those little soundproof room tests.

Or should I say the ones that I didn't always hear. It's funny how the one sound I spent my whole life dreading—the sound that symbolized failure for me because I could never hear them during hearing tests growing up—was the sound to end the silence.

The audiologist had me raise my hand as I heard the beeps, as I had done so many times before. While I raised my hand, she would adjust bars and levels on her computer. Then she turned it off, faced my family, and told them that she was going to turn my processor on and to not overwhelm me with sound.

She assured them that they would each get their own chance to talk to me. Then she turned to me and said, "I am going to turn it on now. You will experience a slight jolt."

She wasn't joking about the jolt. Imagine the feeling of nerves you haven't been able to use suddenly being stimulated with their first surge of information in years. It didn't hurt; it was just an unfamiliar stimulation.

Jolt was the perfect word for her to describe it. Suddenly, my brain was flooded with information. A sense I had been missing was awakened, and my world no longer felt so 2-D. I felt fuller. At this point, I hadn't even heard a real sound. My brain had only received ambient noise, those sounds that are always there but that everyone else tunes out and takes for granted, those familiar friends that remind you that you are never alone.

I couldn't even process them yet. I didn't really understand much more than that they were there. It wasn't until my audiologist said my name and my whole body reacted that I realized that I could hear. It was as if I had been walking in the dark and suddenly found myself in the light.

It was my first sound, my first word, my first time using a dead sense. I felt like I had been awakened, pulled out of this deep dark hole I had found myself in, and brought back out into the world. I cried. I apologized for crying. Then I cried some more. I looked around the room. My audiologist was crying. My mom was trying to hide her tears behind the video camera. But we were all teary-eyed and emotional.

It took a few more seconds before it hit me. This was different; this was wrong. This wasn't what I remembered sound being like. This wasn't beautiful, flowy, comforting, or melodic. This sound was electronic and cold. Yet, as I began to process this new information, my audiologist asked my parents and my little brother, one by one, to say their first words to me.

For the first time in a very long time my mother's lips moved, and they were accompanied by sound. It didn't resemble the voice I remembered from my childhood. But I knew deep inside that what I was "hearing" came from her, even if it was processed by a machine first, and that made it beautiful.

It's hard to describe what hearing through a cochlear implant sounds like to people with the ability to hear because it is such a unique experience. It is such a unique sound that it doesn't exactly relate accurately to anything I have memory of hearing before.

Yet here is my best attempt at describing it. You will probably laugh. When you first have your cochlear implant turned on, before your brain learns each sound again and connects your memories of sounds with the information the machine is providing your brain, everyone who talks, regardless of how deep their voice is, sounds like a robot alien chipmunk.

Yes, you read that right—a robot alien chipmunk. Now use your imagination. Imagine what you think a robot sounds like, what you think an alien sounds like, and what Alvin from *Alvin and the Chipmunks*. Now put them all together. That is what all humans sound like to someone whose implant just got turned on.

It is incredibly amusing. I remember asking random family members to say curse words so that I could hear them through the silly and adorable voices that were coming out of their mouths. It is similar to when kids (and some adults) inhale helium and walk around saying movie quotes or profanities in high-pitched voices.

Relearning Sounds

Eventually my brain started adjusting to all the new sounds around me. I was like a child. Every sound was new to me. Every note, every bang, every ding—all needed to be relearned. I walked around for months tapping things and, in public, asking my family members and friends to identify the sounds happening around us. I was in awe of it all. I was eager to learn everything as quickly as I could. It was like I had been reintroduced to the world.

It started with baby steps. I couldn't magically communicate again. I wasn't a hearing person again. I didn't just remember every sound I had ever heard and go from there overnight. First, I needed to teach my brain how to use this new tool the doctors had provided me with.

I was expected to be able to actually understand words and sentences without any help from lipreading once I got used to it. The idea of someday being able to drive and listen to my passenger tell me about his or her day or even to make a phone call and schedule my own doctor's appointment for the first time made me giddy with excitement. My extended family was excited too.

They all wanted me to hear their voices again and see how this weird device worked. One by one, they came to visit. They spoke, and I laughed. They all still sounded like incoherent robotic alien chipmunks. Try to imagine from my perspective my Uncle Doug, a large broad muscular man who looks like he could hold his own on a football field with the greats, having this tiny little childish voice coming out of that body. It was hysterical.

One evening when we were all celebrating together, I watched as everyone was gathered around the dinner table. My large loud outgoing family discussed something excitedly. They all spoke at once, yelling over each other in a happy playful way.

Everyone had an opinion, and everyone wanted his or her opinion to be heard above the rest at the exact same moment. I smiled as I watched this exchange. I couldn't understand a single word of what was happening in that moment, but I could hear it. I heard the roar of enthusiastic voices begging for attention. I smiled to myself as I sat there. *Level one achieved*, I thought to myself. There was sound. Now I just needed to make sense of it.

A week or so later we were having another family gathering. We had these gatherings at least once a month or so. Roughly twenty of our family members were in attendance. My Auntie Chrissy tapped me to get my attention, and I turned to look at her. "Can you understand words with that thing yet?" she inquired.

"I don't know," I responded as I spun around so my back faced her.

My cousins became quiet all looking on to see what would happen next.

"There is only one way to find out," I continued.

"Say a word, any word."

There was barely a pause before she belted out the word, "Cactus!" with an excited energy.

I swung around with an annoyed look on my face. "Cactus?!" I exclaimed. "Cactus?! You couldn't have come up with a better word for my first word than that?!"

A huge knowing grin spread across her face. I had understood her. I had heard and understood my first word without lipreading!

My cousins all excitedly congratulated me on this accomplishment. *Level two achieved*, I thought to myself as I ran around the house retelling the tale to everyone who hadn't witnessed it.

As time passed, people's voices began to sound like they had in my memory. I started being able to enjoy my mother's voice again, the way her voice gets higher when she is explaining something important and the way her Bostonian accent starts to come out when she is mad.

I started being able to identify sounds like doors opening and closing, honking, and even a phone ringing. Although I was making progress with my implant, I still had to learn and adapt with each new experience as a deaf person.

The implant helped. But it wasn't magic, and it wasn't a "cure." I celebrated every little victory because I deserved those victories. Nevertheless, I was still limited to only some hearing through the implant, and I had a limited understanding of the sounds the world around me was producing.

Soon, I started to perceive more of the sounds around me the way I remembered them, rather than as machine-processed vibrations. These were little things I had never thought I would hear again that had meant the world to me when I was growing up. You see, I never took my hearing for granted as a kid because it was always something I knew could be taken from me at any moment. Growing up, I'd listened to anything and everything I could. I'd absorbed every symphony and every ballad like a sponge. I was improving, learning, and growing with my implant, but there was still something missing—music. After all, a machine can read music, but a machine cannot understand or feel music.

Music is a human experience. My implant was a machine, a machine that couldn't process every sound the human ear can. It is a machine that was programmed to sift through sounds and isolate the ones that it deemed important for me to hear, blocking out all of the "background noise."

I only had about twenty electrodes with which to hear. Hearing people have thousands of cochlear hair follicles with which to pick up sounds. I like to explain my inability to fully process music to people in these terms: Imagine you are looking at a painting, a painting created with tens of thousands of brushstrokes.

All those strokes form the image of a beautiful landscape with rolling green hills. Two cows graze in the background, and a farmhouse stands proudly in the center, glistening in the sun with fresh red-and-white paint and green shutters. Daffodils grow in garden boxes below the two open windows. The barn door is slightly ajar and beckons for you to come inside.

Now imagine you are shown the same painting, only it is actually a picture of that painting through a flip cell phone camera from far away with limited pixel and color options. You may still see a farmhouse. The grass may still be greenish, but the cows are blurred; the farmhouse looks old and tired; and all the details, the individual brushstrokes you could once see that had made you admire and revel in the beauty of the image, are lost. It is the same scene, but it simply isn't the same experience.

At first, music was horrible. It was the most unpleasant thing to hear. It sounded as if someone had thrown some ducks, hyenas, monkeys, and geese in a small pit with a very hungry lion. It was torture for the ears. I had been prepared for the fact that I was never expected to enjoy music again after the surgery. But this was something I never would have been able to accept.

Motivated by either fear or passion, I took out those very same old CDs that I had taught myself to feel music with. I lay across my bedroom floor and played each song over and over and over again, what felt like hundreds of times, with my old CD player turned up to max and my new cochlear implant processor on my head.

If I was ever going to learn to "hear" music again, this was where I was going to start. No one complained about the volume, and no one disturbed me. This was about me and music resolving our differences and learning to love each other again.

Surgery Number 2

A few months after the initial cochlear surgery, I had been having some issues. It started with a soreness, irritation, and redness at the implant site. It became more and more uncomfortable with each passing day.

I complained to my mother about it, but she just thought I was complaining to complain, not actually serious about the pain I was experiencing. One day, I was driving my Auntie PJ to pick up lunch, and all of a sudden, I felt as if I was being electrocuted from inside my skull.

I tried to keep my eyes open, my body tensed up, on the steering wheel and my body started shaking. Tears involuntarily fell from my eyes, and my face took on a look of shear pain. My aunt looked at me concerned and begged me to pull over. I did. I started crying and shaking uncontrollably. I was so scared. My aunt asked what was wrong, and I told her I didn't know. She immediately called my mother and drove me home.

My mother rushed home to meet us. I tried to explain through the pain what was happening. She knew it had to be implant-related, but when she went to pull back my hair to examine the surgery site she was shocked. Not only was the skin covering my implant bright red, but my implant appeared to have shifted. It looked as if it had slid down and embedded itself too close to the top of my ear. A part of the implant was protruding predominately, pushing my thin layer of skin outward.

My dad had been laid off just before the original surgery, and as a result, we were forced to change insurance companies. Seeing the surgeon who had done my surgery was no longer an option. I was lucky though. Our new provider had its own brand-new cochlear implant department.

My mother called the department and made an emergency appointment with its surgeon. He examined me and came to the same conclusion—my implant appeared to have moved. The surgical team would have to cut me open again, examine the implant, and make sure that there were no defects. Then they'd reinsert the implant into a new area of my skull and sew me back up.

After the appointment, the doctor scheduled surgery for that same week. For the next couple days, I sat on my couch in pain and silence. I had dreaded the thought of the first surgery, but I could not wait to have this second one. My mom got me a neck pillow and neck brace. I used them to avoid moving my head and sat motionless on the couch, in fear, counting down the days until my second surgery.

Finally the day of surgery came! This time I had a smaller entourage—my mom, dad, and brother and my Auntie Jayia. I was scared but eager to get it all over with.

The surgery went more smoothly this time. We made sure to talk to the anesthesiologist beforehand to let him know about my last experience with the anesthetic and muscle relaxer.

This time I was given the proper dosage, and since not much of my hair had grown back, they didn't need to shave the side of my head again (silver linings). During surgery, the surgeons observed that the actual implant itself wasn't damaged, so they did not need to replace the piece, just reposition it.

I woke up from the surgery in the recovery room and was able to move this time. It wasn't long before I was able to drink and go to the bathroom. Luckily for me, this time around, the surgery went as smoothly as doctors had told me the first one would go. Soon, I was discharged.

My home recovery time was about the same but less painful. I was stuck, once again, fully deaf, without access to sound, until I healed and could be refitted with my external processor. I experienced a little more dizziness and disorientation this time around through the recovery process, but I looked forward to getting back on my feet and being pain free.

Recovery

When the incision area had healed, I went in for a checkup with my doctor. He said everything looked good and that it was time to have the processor adjusted and turned back on. I was nervous. I didn't know if I would have to start from scratch again and relearn every sound or if I would be able to retain the ability to hear the sounds I had worked so hard to make sense of after the first surgery.

The day the doctors reactivated my implant, I was pleasantly surprised. I didn't go back to exactly where I was before the second surgery, but I didn't have to start from scratch either. This time around, I was even more grateful for every sound because now I had lost them twice in my young life. Retraining my brain to accept the sounds that the implant gave me access to again was a welcomed task, especially since it would be done without pain.

12

TAKE TWO: HEARING ... AGAIN

Reactivation

I still remember hearing rain for the first time since I was a kid. I was up at my parents' cabin in Big Bear, which is a beautiful small mountain community with a breathtaking lake. I loved it there. It was so peaceful away from the busy bustling cities and filled with new nature sounds I had yet to experience with my implant.

I was standing in the kitchen when my processor started to pick up a new sound—almost like a *click, click, click*. I stopped what I was doing and walked all around the cabin trying to find the source of the noise, to no avail.

I turned to my boyfriend at the time and asked him, "What is that noise?!"

He looked at me like I was crazy for a moment and then: "Do you mean the rain?"

My face lit up! I had no idea it was raining outside. I ran to the sliding glass door in the living room and looked out at the heavy rain cannonballing its way down onto the expansive lake.

I was like a kid at Christmas. It was magic. I ran out of the sliding door and stood in the rain with my arms outstretched for a moment, feeling each drop kiss my skin and hearing its brothers and sisters jump into the lake. It didn't sound like rain yet, but I noticed a difference in the vibrations as the water hit the paved sidewalk, the beach, my body, and the lake.

They were different sounds. I began to cry, and my tears joined the raindrops on my face; together they slid down my cheeks. For a moment, I was alone with this beautiful, magical new sound, before I remembered my implant processor isn't waterproof, and I ran back under the cover of the patio, holding onto its wooden support and watching the water hit the lake, completely mesmerized and overwhelmingly grateful.

Every sound felt like a gift from God. Every day, I practiced. Every day, I studied. Every day, I grew stronger and understood more. It felt like it was all building up to this moment.

Soon after, I was sitting in LA traffic, like all LA county dwellers do every day, and a voice came on the radio, my voice. I didn't recognize it at first. Brian's radio broadcast story about me was finally airing! I was parked in gridlock traffic right in front of the cemetery that my Papas is buried in. I rolled down my window and screamed out the window in delight, "Did you hear that, Papa's?! I am on the radio!"

I couldn't actually understand all of what was being said, but it felt euphoric! All the pain and suffering I had been enduring finally had a purpose. *My story could help someone. It could change the life of someone listening at that very moment!* I was filled to the brim with joy. That moment gifted me a feeling of confidence in myself that I hadn't felt in a long time.

So, in typical Amanda fashion, I set out to do everything I was told I "couldn't" do—partially for myself and partially to prove everyone else wrong. I decided to not accept anyone else's limits, that I was going to become a star performer with my implant, and that I was even going to teach myself to sing again.

Breaking Down Barriers

Trying to teach myself to sing again was probably one of the most challenging goals I had ever taken on in my young life. It was even more challenging than calculus. It was also one of the most emotionally trying things I had ever done.

The way my processor worked made it extremely difficult for me to get the information I needed to understand music. It was programed to block out what it considered background noise, and the sound I was getting was unnatural and robotic in a way that was different than what I'd heard through the hearing aids I used to take off and hide in my backpack during my high school choir classes.

In order to understand the music, I needed to hear all the different instruments, not just the ones that my processor decided I should hear. I used a program that was added to my implant that we called "music," which was supposed to turn off the background sound filtering feature when I switched to it.

Even without the filter, every note was slightly distorted. It was almost like everything was sharp or flat. Only instead of all the notes in one given song being either sharp or flat and me being able to adjust my voice for that difference, the way my processor and my brain worked together made the notes in one single song vary between sharp and flat. It was a strange sensation.

My other challenge was that I hadn't used my singing voice in years. I still had some muscle memory, but my vocal tone and trained, clear sound was gone. Like any other muscle in the body, you either use it or lose it, so my voice wasn't anywhere near as good as it had been back when I'd performed with my dad.

It was frustrating at first, trying to find my way through the music. I focused on songs that had been my strengths in high school and quickly discovered that my voice had changed and those low notes that used to be comfortable for me now felt strained. My voice had changed from an alto to a second soprano. I needed to find a way to expand my range again.

I started by working on silly songs to build up my confidence—songs that were fun but didn't have to be sung in a pretty way. I began with getting the beat right, identifying my cues, and starting on the right note. Note matching was probably my biggest struggle. I worked with my friend Andrea and utilized my parents' piano and a tuner app on my phone to practice matching pitch.

The first song I successfully sang was "Popular" from the musical *Wicked.* If you aren't familiar with this song, it's a fun, fast-paced Broadway style number, where the character has a funny high-pitched nasal quality to her voice.

I remember filming myself singing it and replaying it on my phone next to my processor, feeling the vibrations with my hand through the phone case and listening as well as I could with my implant to identify parts of the song that were off or needed fine-tuning.

This became my system. Find a song I was familiar with. Identify the beat. Find a starting note. Use the tuner. Make lots of mistakes. Film rehearsals. Play back the videos to find sections that need more work than others. Practice, practice, practice, and practice some more.

It was frustrating, knowing that this had once come so easily to me. Music had been my thing, and it had just flowed out of me like water before. It was hard accepting that it would always be more difficult for me from now on. It was also difficult to come to terms with the fact that I was nowhere near as good as I used to be.

But I didn't give up. I kept singing and practicing, listening to music through this tool that lived attached to my head because I knew that I was blessed to have any access to sound, and I wasn't going to take that for granted for a single second.

Unfulfilled

A part of me hoped that having the implant would make me happy. That part of me hoped it would reconnect me with my family and the hearing culture I had grown up in and that I would no longer feel different, isolated, or like I was constantly on the outside looking in. It didn't. Even with my new access to sound, I still felt like an alien in the world and culture I wanted to belong to.

Having this new tool didn't change the fact that I was still deaf. It didn't stop me from making people repeat themselves all the time or missing key parts of conversations. It gave me access to some sound on the right side of my head, but it wasn't a 100 percent recovery of my hearing. I still was deaf on the other side of my head, and the sound I was getting on my right was computerized.

I learned that, in loud environments like restaurants, family gatherings, malls, and the like, my processor couldn't figure out what to filter, and all the sounds would just blend together into one loud jumbled mess, making it nearly impossible to hear the voice of whomever was talking to me. This left me feeling just as left out and isolated as I had back in college when I was struggling with my hearing.

This wasn't a fix. This was a tool that was definitely improving my quality of life but wasn't changing the fact that hearing loss was always going to be a part of my life. When I took the processor off at the end of the day, I was still deaf. When the battery died, I was still deaf. When my environment was loud and busy, I was still deaf. It was finally time for me to accept that deafness was always going to be a part of who I am.

I decided to go searching for people like me. I decided to overcome my fear of the "deaf stereotype" and to go searching for the truth. I needed to know other people like me. I needed to know how they lived. I needed an identity. I had been denying and hiding my hearing loss for so long that I had never given myself the opportunity to actually figure out how it was a part of me.

And in failing to do this, I consequently had no idea who I actually was. I went searching for answers to this missing piece of the puzzle. I decided to no longer live ignorantly but to instead learn about my deafness, what it meant, and how it was a part of me.

13

THE QUEST: SEARCHING FOR DEAF PEOPLE LIKE ME

Switched at Birth

Near the end of my college career, a new show aired on TV called *Switched at Birth*. I started watching it around the same time I was losing the very last of my functional hearing. It basically expressed the struggles of a Deaf American teenager who discovered she was accidentally switched at birth with another girl.

It highlights the difference between Deaf and hearing cultures, socioeconomic classes, and other American subcultures. This was the first time I had seen something in the media that I actually felt I could relate to—a deaf young woman who could speak and read lips just like me!

It was a welcomed exposure to Deaf culture. I absorbed every line, every word, and every sign the show showed on TV. I wanted to be Daphne, the Deaf character who was completely accepted by her family and friends, who lived comfortably in both hearing and Deaf environments.

I later learned that Hollywood had glamorized what reality is for a Deaf person, but I am still grateful that this show finally, after years of searching, gave me a Deaf character to look up to—a character who didn't isolate herself from everything I had grown up with and everything I knew.

I hadn't acted in anything since my last mystery dinner show with

C&C Productions, and I was itching to get back on a stage or in front of a camera. I started looking into the show, trying to find out who did casting.

It turned out they weren't casting for any main roles at the time. I found out who was used for background casting and sent an e-mail. The e-mail basically said, "Hi, I'm Amanda. I heard you are casting background actors for *Switched at Birth*. I am deaf and know a little sign language. Please hire me." But it was worded in a slightly more professional way.

Before I knew it, I was scheduled for my first episode as a background actor on *Switched at Birth*. I was so nervous that I reached out to one of my old college friends, from the Deaf group I had attempted to fit in with, to see if he would teach me a little sign language before my first day. By the end of our lunch, I had brushed up on my alphabet and a few short phrases.

When I arrived on set there were two obvious groups—one sitting in one corner of the holding area and another sitting along the opposite wall. One group was signing. The other was speaking English. In that moment, I had a decision to make—stick with the language and culture that was familiar to me but excluded me or take a chance on the language and culture that I wanted to learn about and become a part of.

I took a deep breath, faked a little confidence, and walked over to the "deaf group." Everyone looked up at me expectantly as I stood there hovering above them; I tentatively signed, "Hi. My name A-M-A-N-D-A. I new deaf."

There was a beat and then, one by one, they smiled and signed nice to meet you. They attempted to tell me their names, but I didn't understand most of what they were saying. Even though I was confused and embarrassed by my lack of understanding, I was relieved because they could have just as easily rejected me and sent me over to the other group.

The first girl I met was, like me, raised hard of hearing by a hearing family. She was more comfortable with English than ASL (American Sign Language), had a very light deaf accent, was friendly and approachable, and even had a cochlear implant too! Her name was Raquel.

Once I met her, I stuck with her most of my first day. I did my best to meet everyone else in the group, despite the fact that my knowledge of ASL was basically limited to the alphabet and four other signs. If you ask anyone who met me my first year on *Switched at Birth*, you'll hear about how I followed that girl around like a lost puppy.

It's a running joke, but it is true. I felt like a lost puppy. I was terrified, embarrassed, stressed, and confused every day that I went to work. I did my best to understand the people I surrounded myself with, absorb the culture, learn a new language, and act like I wasn't completely terrified by the whole experience.

Amanda stands with a group of background actors from Deafinit Models and Talent on the set of Switched at Birth in front of the Carlton High School sign.

Sign Language

On set, an interpreter was provided for the group of deaf background actors. She facilitated easy and accurate communication between the English-speaking hearing crew and the Deaf or hard of hearing background cast members. This was my first memory of ever seeing a sign language interpreter in action.

I deviated between reading the lips of the assistant director as he gave instructions and watching the interpreter's hands dance elegantly through the air, forming symbols toward which the other Deaf people on set nodded in understanding. I didn't fully understand either one of them.

I went with the flow, following whoever was closest to me and hoping not to mess up the shot. I quickly learned to identify the signs for "rolling," "background," "action," "cut," and "from the top." These are words and phrases used between each take of a scene, so I saw the hand shapes and motions repeated over and over again and committed them to memory.

In college, I had met a handful of people like me, but at that time, I had been too scared to stick with the exploration of this new culture. This was my first time experiencing a large group of Deaf-cultured people communicating (which is a breathtaking experience, if you have never seen it).

They sat in a large circle between scenes in our holding area. Like King Arthur's round table, it was a circle of inclusion and equality. Everyone had a clear visual of everyone else. There were no obstructions, just a clean open space in the middle of this group of nearly twenty young adult Deaf actors.

It was like watching a symphony. They sat in that circle conversing with people across the way or next to them. Sometimes the conversations included two people. Sometimes the entire circle was involved. They all communicated passionately with not only their hands but also their whole bodies.

Their facial expressions changed with the arrangement of their fingers. Their bodies leaned forward. Their eyes did not waver from their partner in conversation. A dozen exchanges took place at the same time without disturbing or interrupting any other. Hands raised and fell like the dancing fountain in front of the Bellagio in Las Vegas, moving as they exchanged information as if performing an intricate ballet.

The excitement that flowed from their bodies through the tips of their fingers was so mesmerizing that it was hard to tell if they were exhibiting passion or anger as their hands danced around in skilled, lightning fast motions, never missing a beat. It was intimidating to behold but undeniably beautiful.

I found myself staring in awe, trying to decipher this exuberant new code. I cheated, reading lips where I could. However, not all of my Deaf peers moved their lips in English as they signed. I asked those who chose to include me in their conversations to slow their signing down and often stopped them midsentence to mimic a sign they had just perform and ask for its English counterpart.

I was a slow learner, and it took an incredible amount of patience on their part to simply include me in a conversation, but include me they did. Or at least they tried to. I was far from popular on set. Sometimes people would avoid talking to me so that they didn't have to slow down or explain themselves every few seconds. I couldn't blame them. I knew it was as frustrating for them as it was embarrassing for me.

I didn't seem to grow in popularity on set as the weeks and months passed. People talked to me, but I was still the outsider, the girl trying to catch up. I wasn't myself. I was self-conscious about my signing skills, stressed about trying to understand every single sign, and confused by all these cultural rules I had never been exposed to before.

Big D versus little d Deaf

I started to learn that being Deaf didn't simply mean that one couldn't hear. In reality, I learned a truth that shocked me: Most Deaf people *can* hear. Yes, you read that right. I learned that, although all of my Deaf cast mates had significant levels of hearing loss, every person's level of hearing and frequencies of hearing were different. Deaf didn't mean complete silence like I had always assumed it did. In fact, there were three different classifications of people I had previously lumped into the one word, *deaf*. Each group or identity involved not only a person's level of hearing loss but also a person's cultural and language or communication preferences.

At this point in my life I had 100 percent hearing loss in both ears, which medically classified me as "deaf" (notice the lowercase *d*). Yet I was raised in hearing culture, my first language was English, my language preference was English, and I spent most of my time lipreading and trying to fit into "hearing norms," which technically classified me culturally as a "hard of hearing" person.

However, the people I was hanging out with on set, though all of them still had more natural physical hearing than I, identified themselves as Deaf (notice the uppercase *D*). Lower case *d* deaf is a medical classification focused on a level of hearing loss. Upper case *D* Deaf is a cultural classification, identifying a cultural identity and use of sign language as a primary language. I watched as some of my peers jammed to music using an iPod and normal headphones. I saw another one of my peers take a phone call using his "good ear." I had no idea that deafness was so diverse.

I learned that hearing loss did not discriminate. My Deaf peers belonged to every race, every socioeconomic group, and every age range possible, but they were all unified by this one unique human experience called deafness. Some were born Deaf, others became Deaf as children, and many lost their hearing in their teens.

Some had Deaf family members. Some came from hearing families. Many attended Deaf schools, some were mainstreamed, and others were homeschooled. The Deaf community was as diverse as America herself, but the community had its own rules and its own history. It was a painful history of discrimination, persecution, and pain.

Yet from that history, this group of beautiful, courageous people who sat before me had risen like a phoenix from the ashes. I saw the pain in their eyes as they tried to explain to me the trials of their predecessors, family members, and older friends. The name Alexander Graham Bell would bring with it a flicker of anger.

As my peers attempted to explain to me how the Deaf community had become a community, I could see that my suffering, my pain, my constant aching feeling of loss had been felt by the countless Deaf and hard of hearing people who had come before me. Although I was eager to learn, I felt like a burden to my background cast mates. I relied on them for friendship, language, and cultural education. I had nothing to offer them in return for these gifts.

The Struggle

Being around these people was intoxicating for me. I felt like I had found a place where I could finally belong and be accepted. I had never really felt right in an all-hearing world. I decided that I wanted to be able to stand up proudly one day and identify myself as a Deaf person culturally, physically, and linguistically.

This was a shocking revelation for my family, who had watched me put myself through two surgeries in an attempt to get my life in the hearing world back. What they didn't realize was that, even when the implant worked perfectly, I still struggled to communicate and keep up in conversations.

I had fallen back into my old patterns with my family of taking on the burden of communication. They assumed that I was doing great with my new tool. What they couldn't understand is that having this machine in my head didn't make me a hearing person. I wasn't like them. My life was missing something. I was missing an identity.

I figured that, if I became fluent in sign language, my life on set and this transition into my new identity as a Deaf person would go smoother. I heard about these free sign language classes at a church in Anaheim.

I signed myself and my parents up. We went once a week to class, but it was still a struggle to learn the language because, even with the help of the teacher, I still only spoke English in a majority of my everyday communications. On set and one hour a week in class were my only opportunities to use sign language.

This made it challenging to master the language. I would go so long sometimes without seeing any of my Deaf friends and signing (sometimes months) that I was always rusty or forgetting vocabulary I used to have mastered. It was frustrating.

As I tried to educate myself and integrate into Deaf culture, it didn't help that every Deaf person I met already had an established friends group and history with the other Deaf people on set. I was the new girl and a little gullible. The guys sometimes took advantage of that.

Like any language, ASL has lots of language rules that one must learn. The first rule I learned was this: Never trust any of the signs taught to you by the boys on a TV set. This is a lesson I learned the hard way. One day on set, I was reviewing my signs for colors, and I realized I didn't know a sign for *pink*. I turned to the actor next to me and asked him, "How do you sign pink?"

He smiled, made his hand into a letter *P* shape in ASL and tapped it to his nose. For the rest of the week people came up to me and asked what my favorite color was. They were so enthusiastic; I simply thought they were proud of me for learning so much, and I tapped a *P*-shaped hand to the tip of my nose.

It wasn't till one of the actresses on set got offended that I was walking around signing *penis* that I discovered that I had been taught the wrong sign for pink. So when everyone was asking me what my favorite color was, I was enthusiastically replying, "Penis!" It was a harmless schoolboy-type prank, but I was so embarrassed!

At one point on set, I learned that cochlear implants like mine were considered very controversial within the Deaf community. Had I known about all the politics surrounding the surgery, I think I would have been even more stressed about this huge decision in my life.

I discovered that there were many Deaf people (mainly the ones who were lucky to have a Deaf identity, a support system, and access to sign language and Deaf cultural education from a young age) who believed there was nothing wrong with being Deaf. They felt that trying to "fix" us with cochlear implant surgery was wrong and would destroy Deaf culture.

It was all very complicated and involved. Many deaf people, to this day, still hold that belief. I didn't have any access to these people or this point of view at the time of my surgery, but even if I had, I still probably would have made the same decision. I didn't see my implant as a "fix."

The way I saw it, my ears no longer worked well enough for me to use hearing aids like the rest of them. My cochlear implant gave me no more access to sound than their hearing aids gave them. To me, it was just a tool that helped me navigate a hearing-dominated world a little bit more easily.

I had taken all these steps to try to absorb and integrate into deaf culture, yet I had never felt more out of place. When I was around my Deaf friends, I felt like I was acting "too hearing," and every second I was around my family or hearing friends, I felt like I was acting "too Deaf." I couldn't find a balance between the two.

14

MS. INDEPENDENT: TRYING TO FIND MY INDEPENDENCE

Work

Even though I loved working on *Switched at Birth*, the hours and pay were not enough for me to survive off of. So the job hunt continued. After months of searching and applying for jobs that would allow me to utilize my degrees, I ended up applying for a part-time front desk position at a Disney's Grand Californian Hotel and Spa.

I had loved working at Disney during college, so I liked the idea of going back. I remember being able to hide my deafness pretty well at the first in-person interview, thanks to one-on-one communication and a small, quiet controlled environment inside the interview room.

These were ideal conditions for my implant to work at its maximum capacity. The second interview was a little trickier, however. It was a group interview, in a large room were the seats were set up in rows. These were terrible conditions for the use of a cochlear implant processor and lipreading.

I was there early, and I stared at the room in horror thinking of all the challenges I would be facing. What if someone in the row in front of or behind me was answering a question and I couldn't read his or her lips? What if I was asked to add on to someone's response and I hadn't been able to actually understand the response in the first place?

I had prepared myself beforehand with answers to questions

about alternative no cost accommodations (for my deafness) for job requirements like answering the phone and accurately collecting guest information on the job, but I couldn't have planned for this surprise.

I had to think on my toes. Since the interviewer was not in the room yet, I started moving the chairs in the room into a circle and having my fellow interviewees sit in them. I knew a circle would allow me to see everyone's lips clearly and give me my best chance at keeping up with the questions being asked.

When the interviewer entered the room with a surprised look to see all of her candidates in a circle, she asked why we were sitting in a circle. I simply said, "It promotes friendliness and collaboration to sit in a circle, and this way we can see each other and understand each other better."

She nodded, joined the circle, and the interview commenced. After the group interview, I pulled her aside and, in private, let her know that I had hearing loss. I gave her information to ensure her that I could do the job without any extra cost to the company or any hassle.

Because that's what I felt my deafness was when it came to getting a job, a hassle and an inconvenience to employers. I thought that was why I wasn't able to get a job that actually utilized my degree and had to fight so hard for a three-day-a-week, twelve-dollar-an-hour job that didn't require a college education.

To my surprise, I ended up getting the job and started working weekends there. I would still film whenever I was needed on *Switched at Birth*. Even with these two jobs, though, I was having a hard time making ends meet financially. I still had to live with my parents because I couldn't afford the rent anywhere else (yes, my parents charged me rent—cheap rent, but rent).

I also wasn't feeling the sense of pride in my jobs that I wanted to feel. When I told people I worked as a "background actor," they were disappointed. When I told people I worked as a "front desk clerk at a hotel," they were confused as to why I had even gone to college. I wanted to be a lead actor; I wanted a job I could feel proud of, a job that made me feel successful. So, I kept job hunting.

I ended up getting assistance from a rehabilitation organization that helped people with disabilities find jobs. Through the organization, I discovered the incentives the government offers companies to hire people with disabilities in an attempt to help us find employment. It took a while.

I applied for hundreds of jobs and heard back from no one. I was starting to lose faith in myself when I finally got a job as a marketing associate for a local printing and marketing company. It was a small family-owned company, but I was able to negotiate my pay rate up to fifteen dollars an hour.

Being the overly motivated human I am, I worked it out so that I would work Monday through Thursday in marketing, Friday through Sunday at the hotel, and use my sick days to work on *Switched at Birth* whenever the show had scenes for me. I did this for about a year; I worked seven days a week, eight plus hour days, with the occasional twelve- to eighteen-hour day on set.

It was exhausting, but I loved feeling important and busy. I was saving up every penny I could, with the dream of buying my own condo someday.

Yet staying busy was just a distraction from the emptiness and unfulfilled feelings I was having. I started searching for a new agent and submitting myself for acting roles in my very limited spare time. I filmed my auditions at home and sent them in electronically. Acting is 99.9 percent rejection, so I stayed busy with work. I had great friends at my hotel job, took pride in my marketing job, and was growing in my Deaf identity through *Switched at Birth*.

On most sets, everyone looked down on the background actors. We were treated as lesser than everyone else. There were rules in place saying we couldn't take pictures on set, talk to the principle actors, or even get in line for lunch until everyone else had finished getting their food.

Although I understood why these rules existed, they made me feel small on set. It was strange to work for years merely feet from Marlee Matlin, the first and only Deaf woman to win an Oscar for Best Actress, and to have her never notice I existed because, on set, background actors are invisible, merely bodies and blurred colors adding movement to a scene.

I wanted to be seen, I wanted to be acknowledged, and I wanted to be heard. I knew I was a good actress. I just needed the chance to show everyone else what I could do.

At my marketing job, I wasn't invisible. I actually thought my job was cool. We had people and pets. There were three Yorkies; a ferret; a fish tank; and, at one point, some reptiles in my office. There were Segways and even a boxing dummy in the warehouse for letting out that pent-up energy.

Everyone I worked with was supercool. They even tried to teach me Spanish, which I did not end up picking up easily. Yet, I never felt like I truly belonged there. It was a family business. I wasn't family, so I felt weird and a bit awkward. No one there shared my interest in nerdy things or the arts. They all were in sync with one another. I simply didn't fit.

At the hotel, my coworkers were great, but the pay and hours were definitely not something I could survive off of. I liked my job. The people were kind to me, many of my coworkers even showed an actual interest in learning sign language, and I made some pretty great friends!

The hotel was one of the places I faced the most discrimination— not from my coworkers but from guests. One experience that stands out for me happened one night when it was rather slow. Only I and one other employee were manning the front desk. I was at the first computer when a man ran up to my station.

He was half yelling, speaking quickly and looking around while he spoke angrily. By the time I realized he was there and talking to me, he was already partway through his story. I let him finish, trying to gather context clues as to what he could possibly be complaining about from what was left of his story.

When he finished, I responded, "I am so sorry to see you are upset, sir. I apologize, but I missed the beginning of your story. Would you be kind enough to repeat it so I can do my best to help you?"

I didn't even finish this sentence before he was talking fast and angrily again, turning his back to me and pointing in various directions.

Again, I didn't understand him. When his story ended the second time, I calmly and politely apologized for not understanding and asked him to tell me what I could do to do to help him.

Well that set him off even more. He started yelling and throwing his arms around, saying, "No hablo engles? What kind of idiots do they hire for this job?!"

Calmly, I responded with, "Sir, I am sorry you are upset, but I promise you I speak English fluently. I am simply Deaf and need to read your lips to understand you."

To this, he responded, "Why the hell would they hire a Deaf girl? How do you even work? Of course they would hire an idiot deaf girl to work here."

The insults continued. My eyes were filling with tears at this point, and I didn't want to be unprofessional and cry.

I looked away so I wouldn't see any more of the hurtful things he was saying. My coworker had noticed this guy's rant and had gone in the back to get the night manager. The manager appeared and tapped my shoulder to tell me he would take over. I tried to make my retreat to the back room look calm, but I was crying inside.

I walked into the back where one of my coworkers asked me what the guy was so angry about, and I simply responded, "I have no idea."

It turned out one of the rides inside one of the Disney theme parks was closed that day, and he'd decided to complain at the hotel. His complaint had absolutely nothing to do with me, my workplace, or my job. I just happened to be the target of his anger and ableism.

Boyfriend

I worked with some wonderful people and was enjoying having a little spending money in my pocket, but I didn't feel fulfilled. Despite trying to keep myself insanely busy, I felt lonely. I thought that, if I met a guy, then maybe I could fill that emotional void that had been left by my last long-term boyfriend.

I decided to try online dating, and I did meet a guy. At first he was great, but then he started to be not so great. The more I got to know him, the more these little red flags started going off in the back of my head. He was definitely a player, but I figured players could be reformed, and they generally aren't too harmful.

I didn't notice that he was gradually making his way into my head. It started with little put-downs and escalated from there. He had a way of talking me into things I wasn't comfortable with, logically rationalizing behavior that I would normally not allow, and talking in circles in a way that somehow made everything that happened my fault. I went out of my way for him, I changed my behavior and my schedule; cut off my friends; and spent every spare second I had outside of work accommodating him, his schedule, and his wants and his needs and getting nothing in return. The way he spoke to me—the way he always talked down *at* me and never to me—upset my family. Despite being a successful, educated college graduate who was financially stable, I always was made to feel like I wasn't quite good enough around him. The longer we dated, the worse it got. I didn't even notice the beginning signs of mental abuse until the night he physically shoved me at a public event for politely introducing myself to a girl he used to hook up with.

There was a kind young woman there who had seen him shove me and noticed the signs of abuse before I did. She offered to get me out of the situation and give me a ride home. If I were ever to see her again, I would give her a big hug and say thank you. At the time, I turned down the ride.

The stress of the relationship, the work hours, and the feeling of being unfulfilled were starting to physically wear me down. I became ill and got shingles from the sheer weight of it all. My doctors even advised me to break off my relationship and cut down on my hours.

Then my boyfriend said something to me, after I asked him to hold a camera so I could film a quick audition, before we left. "Why? You aren't going to be successful at this," he said. "If you were actually serious about it, then you would quit your job and focus 100 percent of your attention on acting." He said it in a way that was just cruel enough to hurt me and make me doubt myself but in a tone that a passerby wouldn't have been able to identify as malevolent.

Yet it was true. I sat with that thought for a little and decided that this one sentence was all this guy was ever going to positively contribute to my life. I was so ashamed. I had always thought of myself as a strong young woman who would never let a guy treat her that way. The mental abuse didn't happen overnight; it was so gradual I didn't even see it coming.

I knew he had grown up in an abusive household, and my empathy for his rough childhood had made me blind to the fact that he was slowly recreating that environment for me. I felt so pathetic to have fallen for his charms. I felt weak and out of control of my own life.

I tried to break up with him, but he wouldn't let me. For weeks, I struggled to break his control over me, until finally I gathered enough self-worth to resist his silver tongue and cut him out of my life.

Just a few days after our breakup, he had a new girlfriend. On one hand, I was relieved to be free of him. On the other hand, his ability to jump immediately into a new relationship hurt me. I remember finding out while surrounded by friends and not being able to stop myself from crying. He had made me feel weak when I was with him, and now only a few days later, he'd made me feel worthless, replaceable.

I was amazed by how time and time again men (boys really) could treat me like a plaything to be tossed out and forgotten about. They just left me and immediately moved on to some new girl.

I was starting to wonder if I would ever learn how to pick better guys. Or more importantly, I wondered if I would ever gain back all the self-respect and self-worth these last couple boyfriends had emphatically drained from me.

I took my ex's advice and decided my dreams deserved my full attention. I decided that I didn't want to wake up one day and be eighty years old in a rocking chair wishing I had really tried to make it as a successful actress. So I took a leap of faith. I quit my jobs and threw myself into acting to find fulfillment and love for myself.

It was terrifying to take such a huge risk for a dream. All I had was my small amount of savings, a digital camera, a room in my parents' house about an hour outside of LA that I rented for three hundred dollars a month, and a dream.

15

A WHOLE NEW WORLD: LEARNING TO LIVE AS A DEAF PERSON

The Deaf Community

O nce a year, the streets in downtown LA are blocked off for Deaf Day LA. The street is lined with colorful canopies, each representing a different Deaf-owned or Deaf-friendly business. There are musical performances, dance performances, storytelling in sign language, short scenes, stand-up comedy, and even a fashion show at night after the sun goes down.

Hundreds of Deaf people, CODAs (Children of a Deaf Adult), hard of hearing people, interpreters, students, and people who have no hearing loss or connections to the Deaf community at all come out to enjoy the festivities. If you have never been to a Deaf event, go. It doesn't matter if you have perfect hearing and don't know a single word in sign language, going to a Deaf event will change your perception of the word *disabled*.

I have never seen a group of people more diverse, lively, and social. Plus, in my experience, Deaf people really know how to let go, party, and have a good time. Growing up, I had no idea that such a rich and vibrant culture existed as a sanctuary for people just like me.

My first time at an all-Deaf event was a little overwhelming at first. I didn't know what to do, who to talk to, or where to go. The large Fairplex exhibition space was filled with hundreds of people grouped sporadically in circles having excited conversations in sign language nearly everywhere you turned.

Yet the exhibition building lacked that familiar overwhelming loud echo that one would expect when a building is filled with hundreds of people all talking at once. It wasn't completely silent. The sounds of hands randomly clapping together, a laugh, a sigh, or a few words could be heard now and again through my cochlear implant processor.

Becoming a member of the Deaf community gave me a sense of identity and a support system. I now had access to information, accommodations, technology, friends, and advocates that I'd never had before. The community taught me my legal rights as a person with a disability. My new friends showed me how to request an interpreter and how to stand up for myself. They taught me that my deafness wasn't something to be ashamed of. It wasn't a curse or a punishment, as I had believed it to be as a child. It didn't make me weak or rob me of my independence.

It wasn't something to be pitied but, instead, understood. My deafness was my new beginning, my ticket into a whole new vibrant world. It was my strength. My deafness hadn't taken from me. It had given me gifts—the gift of empathy, understanding, heightened awareness, kinship, and strength.

It had given me a community, a language, and an identity. For the first time in my life, I was able to proudly say I was Deaf. I could accept the piece of myself that I had fought for so long. For the first time in my life, I felt supported and no longer alone.

Changes

Now that I had accepted my identity, how I was going to live as a "Deaf person" was still a question that lingered in my mind. Yes, I was Deaf, and yes, I was living, but I hadn't decided what parts of the culture

I was going to implement in my daily life. I know that sounds weird, but it was what was happening.

You see, there is no one way to be Deaf. There is no right or wrong way to live as a Deaf person. There are lots of lifestyle choices I had to make. I had to decide what parts of my old culture I would keep and what parts of the new culture I would adopt.

Sign language was, by far, the better form of communication for me. However, I was limited to using it with others who already knew it. Those were few and far between. I had to find a way to incorporate my deafness into the hearing-dominated world I so badly wanted to be successful in.

At the same time, I didn't want to limit myself or my career with this new title or let my deafness define me based on society's warped and inaccurate understanding of what "deaf" means. I wanted to make my own way and be successful on my own terms. My mother kept reminding me that I was an actress who "happened to be Deaf," but it was up to me to actually establish what that meant and looked like.

My friends, Raquel and Arleta, played a big part in helping me figure this all out. We each had our own unique way of being Deaf and of communicating with the hearing world around us. One weekend, we decided to have a girls' weekend in Las Vegas. My dad named it "Deaf Girls Gone Wild Weekend," but it was pretty chill.

The most interesting thing for me about that weekend was seeing how unique our three styles of living as Deaf women were. For example, we went to grab some sandwiches for lunch our first day in Vegas, and we stood in line with everyone else at Earl of Sandwich located inside the Planet Hollywood Casino and Hotel.

When I got up to the cash register, I spoke my order in English. The cashier asked me a few follow-up questions, which I had him repeat once or twice as I lip-read to the best of my ability, and then I moved down the line.

Next, Raquel came up to the cash register. She pulled a piece of paper and pen out of her bag, wrote her order on it, and then handed it to the cashier. In English, the cashier asked a follow-up question. She read his lips and then wrote her response to his question on another piece of paper.

Last up was Arleta. She pulled out her phone and typed her order. She then turned the phone around and showed it to the cashier. He asked her a question in English, and she gestured for him to use the receipt paper from his machine to write his question. He figured it out and wrote down, "Would you like anything else?" clearly on the paper. She shook her head indicating no and then joined us farther down the line.

We each had our own ways of communicating with the hearing-dominated world around us. Each option had its pros and cons. I was still trying to find a balance with my way of communicating. You see, because I spoke well and lip-read, people tended to not realize that I could not hear.

This caused me more problems than it solved most of the time. People started to become frustrated with me easily, they yelled at me, or the exchange would become so confusing or embarrassing for me that I was forced to explain to them that I was, in fact, Deaf.

If I resorted to using the "D word," they typically reacted one of five ways. They either called me inspirational; became scared of communicating with me; told me I spoke well "for a deaf person"; pitied me; or felt the need to tell me some story about how their sister's friend's stepbrother's dog was deaf in one ear, and as a result, they knew exactly what my life was like. It was exhausting.

People Were Afraid of Us

It wasn't until I spent some time with my Deaf friends in public, using only sign language, that I started to notice how differently the world was reacting to us. When I hid my hearing loss and spoke and lip-read to communicate, I typically was treated well by strangers.

Granted, I grew up a middle-class white girl. I had a lot of unspoken privilege. I knew what discrimination was, but I had no idea what it felt like, because I had never actually experienced it. For the first time in my life, I walked down the street with my friends and people stared. They actually physically went out of their way to cross the street to avoid us. They pointed, made comments, and even took pictures.

I felt like a sideshow, a pariah. My friends appeared oblivious to these reactions as we continued walking, maybe because they were used to them.

Arleta, Amanda, and Raquel take a selfie together.

We went to a restaurant for dinner together one night. It was one of those restaurants where the tablecloths are paper and you can draw on them with crayons. After we were seated, we picked up the crayons and wrote our drink orders on the paper tablecloth where the waiter would have been clearly able to see them. We waited, catching up with each other enthusiastically in sign language.

Thirty minutes later, no one had even come over to take our drink order. I tried to wave someone down politely, and they pretended not to see me. Then I saw the waiters near the kitchen playing rock–paper–scissors. After three games, the loser reluctantly sulked over to our table, and in a loud overexaggerated voice, yelled, "*What ... do ... you ... want ... to ... drink?*"

We politely pointed to the written drink order on the tablecloth. He read it and hurried away. We wrote our food orders down in the same area of the tablecloth and waited for his return. But instead he sent someone else to the table with our drinks a few minutes later.

We waited and waited until eventually he came back; looked at the tablecloth; copied our orders onto his notepad; and, without so much as looking at us, walked away. This time, we waited about a half an hour for our food to come to the table. No one checked on us, and our drinks remained empty, with no hope of being refilled.

At around twenty dollars a plate, we expected better service. I looked over toward the kitchen and saw all three of our plates just sitting there, though I had no idea how long they had occupied that space. I waited to see what would happen. We had been sitting in that booth for over an hour in a famous chain restaurant that was more than half empty.

Many waiters hung around the kitchen area talking. The table next to us, who had arrived after us, had already finished their meals and had been granted multiple refills by the same waiter. Yet we sat there, hungry, thirsty, and waiting. About fifteen minutes later, our food still hadn't moved.

I got up and started walking toward the kitchen to pick up the plates myself. Then our waiter jumped into action, grabbed them, and walked them hurriedly to our table. He dropped them off and turned on his heels, not even giving us the opportunity to ask for refills of our empty drinks.

My pasta was cold, but my friends were not complaining, so I sucked it up and ate the food I had. This may have been the first time it happened, but this experience in public places and restaurants started to become a pattern. People didn't want to serve us. If I didn't use my voice, I couldn't expect good or even semidecent service. Instead, I would be brushed off or forgotten about.

It wasn't just individuals; companies, organizations, and groups of people began revealing their ignorance about deafness to me on a more frequent basis. It was interesting because I had become more open about my deafness in public and more aware of how little the public understood about disabilities.

It was like being awakened from the Matrix but going back in on a mission and not being able to find a phone to get out.

Accepting my identity definitely shook up my public life, but it made my private life better. I was able to utilize the resources the community had given me to improve my sign language communication and my home life. I now had a doorbell that made lights flash so that I would know when someone was at the door.

I had a CapTel phone (a phone that captions what the person on the other line is saying) so that I didn't need to rely on my cochlear implant processor all of the time. I got a vibrating alarm clock to wake me up in the morning. I also got Purple technology added to my cell phone and TV, allowing me to communicate with my Deaf friends via video phone, make sign language-interpreted calls, and connect with Deaf resources and businesses from my home.

Not to mention being introduced to websites with information like captionfish.com, which showed me where all open captioned and closed-captioned movies were showing in theaters across America, giving me more access and choices to watch films in theaters like everyone else. There were dozens of things that the community introduced me to that helped make everyday activities easier.

Family Matters

I was still trying to figure out who I was as a Deaf woman though. I was all over the place in my communication. I was tired of being the one burdened with having to lip-read or always wear my processor just to have a simple conversation with my immediate family members.

Sometimes at home, I would refuse to speak, in an effort to force my family to learn sign language so that we could more efficiently communicate with one another. Other times, I would poorly attempt to sign and speak at the same time to get them engaged in seeing the word in sign language and hearing it in English.

Other times, I would simply give up, speak, and lip-read. My mom was attempting to learn the language, but she wanted to rely on me for all of her practice. I was still at a beginner level. I was not consistent enough with what language I chose to use at home for her to even really become fluent.

She didn't have other Deaf friends, like I did, to practice with. So even though she went to a free, once-a-week sign language class at church, her signing was limited to the ABCs and a few descriptive words. My mother brought my father with her to the weekly sign language class. He sat through them dutifully, but he had gotten it into his head that he was too old to learn sign language and that his hands "just couldn't" form the signs. He never really picked up more than a handful of words.

Occasionally, he would try to make up his own, but they would always come out looking awkward or offensive. My brother was away at USC through this transitional period in my life. He didn't get to see most of my struggle with my identity; his focus was school.

My grandmother, who was there every step of the way, outright refused to learn any sign language. She claimed that she was afraid my speech would start deteriorating again if I stopped speaking and started using my hands to communicate with her. She didn't realize how much exhaustion, frustration, and strain on my eyes lipreading created.

It hurt. I felt like I wasn't important enough to my immediate or extended family for them to try to communicate with me better. First I blamed myself. Maybe I had made it too easy for them by being so good at lipreading and talking all of these years. Maybe I still hid my pain too well.

Maybe if I had been less stubborn as a child and admitted I needed help, they would have learned for me then, even though they wouldn't now. They insisted they loved me but continued to choose to ignore my struggles. They continued to ignore my deafness. But it was a part of me now.

It was a part of who I was, and I was not going to hide it or fight it anymore. I was trying to learn to live in harmony with it. All I wanted was for the people I loved to accept that. They still thought of deafness as a weakness, a disability, and a burden at a time when I was finally seeing my deafness for what it truly was—an unchanging part of me. I realized that being deaf is not a negative thing, just like having brown hair isn't a negative thing. It is just a fact of my being.

16

THE OBSTACLE COURSE: OVERCOMING SETBACKS

I was finally settling into my identity. My cochlear implant was helping me successfully function in a hearing-dominated world. I was following my dreams. I was in excellent shape. Life finally seemed to be falling into place for me.

Car Accident

One day, I was on my way to a meeting for a new project in development. It was a pilot show being created to be pitched to PBS. I had picked out this adorable lacy white dress and strappy wedges. I was so excited. The show would allow me to share my hearing-loss story, in hopes that it would help others to be inspired to overcome their own personal obstacles.

Then fate decided to test my resilience again. It was September 9, 2014. I was sitting in my car in stopped LA traffic, like every other day, when I felt the first impact. A Lexus had rear-ended me. I remember thinking, *Dang, now I am going to be late for my meeting*—just before the second more violent impact threw my body forward.

My cochlear implant processor dislodged from my head and was chucked onto the floor of my car. The back of my head collided with my headrest. My head was buzzing, everything was blurry, my heart was beating so fast I thought it would explode from my chest, and my whole body was shaking uncontrollably.

I took deep breaths and managed to feel around on the floor until I found my cochlear implant processor. I stuck it back on my head and pulled my damaged car over to the carpool lane just over to my left. That's when a truck viciously collided with the center divider a few feet in front of my car, sending my heart into a second furry of palpitations.

I was scared and in shock. This one truck had managed to hit four cars (mine included), creating a horrible accident that shut down the 60 Freeway. My car was one of the lucky ones, it was still in one piece, but the trauma to my head changed my life and my hearing once again.

The police had to temporarily close the freeway to get us off—a pathetic parade of damaged cars doing their best to drag themselves across a stopped freeway to the emergency lane.

I remember having to explain to each paramedic, cop, and concerned citizen who came to my door to check on me that I was Deaf and that I needed to read their lips. Communicating was hard with my head injury. It didn't even occur to me to ask for a sign language interpreter. I am not even sure if I would have felt completely comfortable communicating in sign language at this point in my life.

Somehow, I managed to stumble through all of this important communication on my own. It took all my willpower to simply focus on people's lips, and I was seriously struggling to understand what everyone around me was saying. I continued to be disoriented and dizzy.

I was physically shaking; driving off that freeway was hard. My mom was there at the off-ramp waiting for me, after getting my text about the accident and running out the door in the middle of a mani-pedi to be there for me. The second my mom saw me, she knew that there was something wrong with me.

She rushed me to the emergency room. I was so tired while we sat in that waiting room—still in the pretty lace dress and heels I had picked out for the television meeting I was supposed to attend in LA. It was cold. My mom and I waited for hours and hours.

It took all of my strength just to stay awake as I slumped in the uncomfortable chair staring in the direction of the TV but not really taking anything in. I was wrapped in a blurry cocoon. Nothing was in focus. I felt like I wasn't really there. It felt almost like I was in a dream. The only thing that told me this wasn't a dream was the intense pain in my head that was draining away the little energy I had left.

Finally they called me. There was no sign language interpreter available, so all of my communication with the doctors went through my mom, as usual. After a CT scan and X-rays, it was determined that I had a severe concussion, along with neck and spinal strain. I was sent home with some painkillers.

I was surprisingly positive about it all; I am good with pain and suffering for some reason. Being in physical pain brings out strength in me that I can't explain. I excel at getting through tough medical situations; I probably would have gotten through this one very gracefully had the damage been limited to a simple concussion, headaches, and spinal strain. I would have very happily taken my ibuprofen, watched Netflix, and gone to physical therapy. I was not that lucky though.

Within about forty-eight hours after the accident, the electric-type shocks started. My implant seemed to be damaged. The machine in my head that was supposed to improve my life by giving me back some of my hearing had turned against me and was determined to roast my brain like a marshmallow.

I was helpless as these sharp, painful shocks attacked the right side of my brain. It felt like I was being electrocuted from the inside out. The jolts were accompanied by the feeling of three-inch needles being slowly inserted into my skull around the implant site. My whole body would react to the shocks; it would tense up, and I would jump or move uncontrollably. It was indescribably painful.

The days that followed were worse, filled with intense, unbearable migraines, which would make me cry uncontrollably, lose my ability to tell what direction was up, and fall to the ground. Sometimes I would start shaking uncontrollably. My days were dizzy, painful blurs of doctor's appointments, physical therapy, and Netflix.

I couldn't drive, I couldn't focus, and I couldn't function. My dad, who had gotten laid off the same week as my car accident, and my mom, drove me everywhere. They watched me suffer as the doctors misdiagnosed me, saying it was a just a bad concussion and telling me to take more pain meds. I went to neurologists and specialists, and everyone seemed to dismiss my pain. They seemed to just brush me off as some whiny little girl who couldn't handle a headache.

The migraines never ceased; my head pounded and ached twenty-four hours a day, seven days a week. Sometimes my vision was blurry. Sometimes I could barely walk because just moving my head was unbearable. I handled the pain the best I could. Pain medication didn't help at all. The embarrassment, however, was difficult for me to bear.

I distinctly remember one afternoon when I was so dizzy and my head was in so much pain that I swore my ears would start bleeding any second. My world all of a sudden was flipped upside down. I felt like I was on a ship in the ocean in the middle of a tornado. I collapsed.

Next thing I knew I was flat on the floor, my mom was holding my head in her hands, my aunt was checking my body for wounds, and I was crying hysterically. I was just so tired of living in constant pain that I couldn't stop the tears. I kept screaming, "Make it stop! I can't take it anymore!"

Just at that moment, my younger cousin walked in the room to witness the scene. I remember most distinctly the look of horror in her eyes as my grandmother guided her away from the room.

Silence Part 3

My mom took me back to the specialist where I'd had my first implant surgery. I was terrified my implant had been damaged; it was the only explanation I could think of for everything I was going through. Just the thought of having another surgery made my eyes start to water. I didn't know if I could emotionally or physically handle another one.

Another CT scan was ordered, once the swelling of my brain (from the concussion) went down. I was then sent to see what the cochlear implant audiologist could do for the electric shocks as far as processor adjustments, to make me more comfortable.

My audiologist saw me that very same day also. She hooked me up to her computer and began testing each electrode individually. When she got to the first one causing the shocks, my whole body jumped. I screamed, "*Stop!*" and tears swelled up in my eyes.

She quickly deactivated that electrode with her computer, which immediately stopped the shocks but also left me with less access to sound. She offered to stop the testing, but I insisted she continue. I knew I needed as much hearing as I could save to function at work, with my family, and with my friends, but the pain from the shocks had to be assessed.

My body was attacked by this intense, unbearable pain three more times before she finished her tests. She turned off four electrodes in my cochlear implant that day; this stopped the painful shocks and eased the migraines a bit but left me with barely enough hearing to function.

Imagine waking up after fighting so hard, losing your hearing twice, suffering through two surgeries, and handling two recovery periods with surprising strength just to once again be unable to hear your mother's voice, use a phone, order a burger at a drive-through, or even hold a conversation with a stranger. I was only twenty-four. I was supposed to be enjoying life and my youth, but it was starting to seem like I would never catch a break long enough to actually have any "normal" youthful experiences.

Depression

The physical damage was intense, but the emotional toll was unbearable. After the accident, I began to suffer from depression. It was real depression, not just sadness. This was a different, all-consuming pain, worse than I could have possibly imagined. It felt unmanageable at times; I would look in the mirror and not recognize the person staring back at me.

On the days I woke up depressed, the girl in the mirror's eyes were so cold and harsh-looking. There was no cheerfulness, none of that familiar innocent optimism sparkling in them. There was hatred in those eyes—not for others; it was a hatred reserved for me.

I tortured myself by replaying memories of my past and current failures, over and over again in my mind.

Even my skin seemed grayer somehow, almost dead. I barely moved from the couch, and I was trapped inside my body somewhere, trying to will myself into a better mood, trying to prove to myself that I had some worth left. Yet every day I would eventually give up and just sit there feeling hopeless, helpless, and useless, adding another failure to the memories that would play in my head the next day.

The pain of adapting to a loss of my hearing again, while surrounded by only hearing people, on top of all of this was just too much for me to handle sometimes. My depression made me feel weak and isolated me from my friends. Once again, I found myself a lone Deaf person.

All of my Deaf friends were out in LA. I was trapped, without the ability to transport myself from Pomona. I felt like I was quarantined from people like me and stuck in a world that saw my hearing loss as yet another weakness. My depression started warping my view. With the loss of sound from my processor, I was barely functioning.

No one around me knew sign language well. The intense migraines I suffered from after the concussion made it nearly impossible for me to lip-read. I started to resent my deafness again. Being apart from the hearing world around me, being unable to communicate, being looked down upon, and being pitied killed me. I had worked so hard to understand as much as I could with my implant.

Even though it had provided me with imperfect sound, I missed it. Before the accident, I had been able to understand full sentences with my processor on. Now, I could no longer understand a single word; I just got jumbled sounds that started and stopped. The frequency that held my mother's voice had been lost when they turned off the painful electrodes, and it broke my heart to watch her lips move and try to imagine her voice again, like I had in college.

I could no longer hear children laugh or cry. Music was out of reach for me once again. The sound of rain, which I had treasured since that moment in the cabin, was stolen from me. It felt like a dagger to the chest. I had grown up in hearing culture, so naturally I wanted to fit in.

I was angry, to say the least. I was frustrated. I was pissed. My implant hadn't made me a hearing person, but when it had worked, it had definitely made my life easier in this predominantly hearing world. The Deaf part of me felt guilty for wishing my processor would work again.

A part of me was still proud to be Deaf. But at the same time, I wanted to be able to simply talk to my family. I also wanted to give myself my best chance at achieving my dreams and functioning independently in a world built on hearing dependence. I was so conflicted.

I would go into auditions and once again be unable to understand those around me. I looked stupid if I tried to hide my "disability" and asked them to repeat themselves a million times. Yet if I said I was Deaf, I was met with looks of pity, and I would lose any chance I had of booking the role.

After all, my depressed mind reasoned, why would anyone hire the Deaf girl when a hundred other actresses who looked exactly like her and could do the job without the added financial costs of an interpreter on set were lined up in the waiting room?

The latest string of failures was killing me. I knew I was a good actress, able to do the jobs I was auditioning for. Yet, the anxiety I would feel as I walked into that audition room, attempting to read new casting agents' lips each time, would throw me off. I couldn't live like this any longer—being in these rooms with people who could make all of my dreams come true, standing there and staring them in the face, failing to understand them, and not giving the type of performance I knew I was capable of as a result.

For nearly two year, I struggled with these irrational anxieties and dark, negative thoughts that swam through my mind on a daily basis. I fell deeper and deeper into a depression as I watched more and more doors slam in my face, more and more doctors tell me they couldn't help me, and more and more opportunities pass me by. I felt like giving up. I had suicidal thoughts.

But I was still me; I was not capable of giving up. Being a fighter was hardwired into the most basic fabric of my DNA. Life may do everything in its power to put me down, but I always find a way to lift myself back up—because I am worth the struggle.

Overcoming

I didn't recognize myself anymore. I was a shell of a person. Per my usual pattern, I isolated myself and distanced myself from everyone who loved or cared for me. I couldn't let my loved ones see me suffer. I lost some great friends and strained some strong relationships in an attempt to never let anyone see me weak.

I knew I needed to turn my life around. My depression was running my life. I knew that how I was living wasn't helping me get any better, but no one ever accomplishes such things alone. Sometimes we need to know when to ask for help. So I swallowed my pride and did exactly that.

I finally confessed to those close to me that I was struggling. Surprisingly, they lined up to show their support without passing judgment.

Having my family and friends back was a great start, but I could see how the change in my mood and personality was affecting them.

I was very negative; nearly everything that came out of my mouth dragged the conversation down. I was obsessed with my own suffering. I knew I needed to get some of my old optimism back if I was going to keep the people I cared about. So I made a list of the things I complained about the most.

Many of the items on my list were related to the loss of my hearing, postconcussion symptoms, migraines, and depression, which were things only time could heal. But also on that list were my weight and appearance. I had let myself go. I had gained a lot of weight since the accident, due to inactivity and overeating.

I hadn't been eating well or doing general female maintenance things, like eyebrow tweezing or regularly doing my hair and makeup. I decided to take control of the things I could change. I decided to start working out and building myself a stronger body. I figured, if I could lose some weight and get myself one victory, it might give me the confidence to tackle something bigger.

I remember the first day of my new outlook on life; I willed myself out of bed and into my sweatpants and went to the gym in Diamond Bar. I was so self-conscious, I had bought large baggy gym clothes that hung off my body and hid every curve. My shirts hung down past my butt, and I pulled them down farther every few seconds in an effort to hide my thighs.

Since I was a kid, I had struggled with my weight; it had been an ongoing battle for me, and it had always been an insecurity. I wrote about my first time trying Weight Watchers in my diary when I was only eleven years old. I watched my mom and aunts try diet after diet trend and never succeed to keep off whatever they did lose.

It was a family battle. But as an actress, who Hollywood expects to look a certain way, I felt even more pressure to shed some pounds. Before the accident, I had finally reached my ideal body goals. I weighed a little over 120 pounds and was more muscle than fat. I had a thin waist, a flat stomach, toned legs, and strong arms. It had taken me almost two years after the steroid treatments and cochlear implant surgeries of counting calories and working out five times a week, but I had finally gotten to a point where I felt comfortable wearing shorts and fitted tops. I felt I looked great! I missed that version of my body. I missed feeling strong, healthy, and happy.

Even though I had always struggled with my weight, this time was different. This time, the extra weight came from loss of control of my life, my health, and my happiness. This time I needed to succeed to live.

I started going to every gym class the gym offered at 8:30 a.m. At first, the classes were hard. Sometimes my migraines would cause me to have to sit out a set or two. But no matter what, I kept trying, and I kept going.

The young man who ran the check-in desk at the gym discovered that I was Deaf one day as I came in. The next day when I walked in, he finger-spelled the word "hi" to me. I was shocked and shyly waved "hi" back. The next day, he had learned how to sign "Good morning" and showed me as I walked in.

Each day, I was greeted with a new a sign, and each day, I felt stronger than the last. Little by little, as my body changed, so did my mood. My body was getting stronger, and I was becoming more positive. I could now at least fake a smile, and I finally had some energy to do things instead of sleeping away my days.

Most people, when faced with internal struggles, turn to religion for answers. Whether you are Catholic, Buddhist, Jewish, Muslim, or Christian, we all need a little spiritual guidance every once in a while. So, I sought out God to help me find my inner strength.

I went back to the Catholic Church I had been raised in looking for peace and guidance. I was looking for something to fill this hole that had developed in my chest. I needed a direction.

I didn't find it there. You see, I had grown up in that church. I could sit, stand, and kneel at all the right times. Yet this place that used to be a sanctuary for me felt empty. It wasn't because I was no longer a believer but because I could no longer connect with the message. Losing my hearing had made me an outsider in my church. No one knew sign language, there were no interpreters at Mass, and I couldn't communicate effectively there anymore. I sat through Mass after Mass in silence, sitting and kneeling and standing at all the right times and saying amen and reciting prayers when I was supposed to. But it all felt simply routine; it had lost its meaning to me.

That emptiness in my chest was still there. I knew I couldn't give up on myself or on God. So in a half-assed effort, I posted on Facebook asking a friend if her church had sign language-interpreted services. She replied back, "Yes!" So together we planned to go to her church that following Sunday. I was so nervous.

It was a Christian church. I had never been to a Christian Mass. I had been attending the same Catholic Church for twenty years. I was also worried my sign language skills would not be strong enough to get me through the sign language-interpreted Mass.

As I walked in, I noticed an immediate difference. People were dressed in street clothes rather than their Sunday best, and the pews were replaced with rows of gray, padded chairs. In place of the ornate mission-like walls covered in paintings of Christ's life story with brightly colored stained glass windows depicting saints, there were plain warehouse-style walls and very few windows. Where the ornate stone alter decorated in brightly colored cloths, flowers, and grand golden candlesticks topped with gold-inlaid candles would be, there was a simple raised wide platform, decorated with three simple banners and covered in musical instruments. There was a small podium at its center. There was no full choir, but there were large screens on each side of the stage and camera equipment positioned in the audience, whose images appeared on the large screens.

When we arrived, we walked to the very front of the large church. The first two rows had signs reading, "Reserved for Deaf Ministry." I took a seat in the first row and my friend sat behind me as an upbeat rock-like melody started on the stage.

A full band with a drummer, a bass player, a guitarist, a pianist, and three singers played. The worshippers around me stood and swayed with the music. Some waved their hands in the air and praised as they sang the words along with the band.

The interpreter sat at the base of the stage a few feet in front of me. Her short brown hair and welcoming smile didn't question my belonging. Instead, she gave me a welcoming nod as her kind eyes locked with mine and her hands began to gracefully dance along with the upbeat music.

The words formed by her hands also appeared on a large screen up above her. The church signs she produced that were foreign to me were clearly written in black and white right above her.

I was so used to chants, wearing my Sunday best, receiving communion, and kneeling and standing that this was a bit of a culture shock for me. But for the first time in forever, I had full access to the songs being sung in church. Eventually, the pastor took the stage. He was a kind-looking middle-aged man with an approachable demeanor.

He looked like he would just walk off the stage at any moment and start patting people's backs, calling them "buddy," and talking about last night's game. He began preaching, and as I followed along with the interpreter's hands, I saw the signs for *God, Jesus, amen,* and *pray* for the first time in my life.

My friend watched as my eyes watered and stared in awe as Bible verses displayed themselves on the large stadium screens. To have this kind of access to anything was overwhelming for me. I was so grateful I felt I would burst. I could hardly handle the joy of being included, of being thought of, of being understood.

I later came to the realization that one of my biggest problems was that, through all of these hardships, I had lost sight of my dream. I had lost the thing that gave my life meaning, got me up in the morning, and kept me moving forward. I needed to reevaluate my dream. So I did.

I sat down and made a list of all the things I was grateful for. I made a list of all the things I wanted to achieve. I made a list of all the people I wanted to help. I made a list of what makes me happy. After making all of these lists, I came to the same conclusion I had when I was four years old. I wanted to be a successful actress.

Acting made me happy. It would be able to give me the platform to inspire and encourage positive change. My passion also had the potential to give my voice power, to make people want to listen to me, and to make my voice heard by millions more than I could dream of reaching in my current situation.

If I succeeded, I could make life better for minority groups, like the Deaf and disabled community, whose voices were often ignored. I knew what I wanted to do. Now I needed to create a plan to achieve that goal; I made a plan. I created smaller achievable goals and dates I hoped I could reach them by.

Then I created smaller daily goals, and every day I did one or two things that would help me get one step closer to those goals. I did things like submitting myself for roles, forcing myself to get out of the house and go to networking events, having new headshots taken, joining an auditioning class, and creating my own short films and YouTube videos.

Focusing on this gave me a sense of purpose, my daily achievable goals gave me a sense of accomplishment, and the help of my doctors and the right medication helped clear my head. Day by day, my life started to get better, my goals became clearer, my relationships became stronger, my body became toner, and my faith was restored.

Change of scenery

I still felt stuck. I decided that a change of scenery might be just what I need to bring me back to myself. My brother graduated from USC with a bachelor of science in electrical engineering in June 2015 and immediately was offered a job in aerospace.

He decided he wanted to see the world before surrendering to a desk job for the rest of his life, so he started planning a trip to Europe. After asking all of his friends if they wanted to accompany him on the trip and being turned down or blown off, he finally invited me along.

We immediately started budgeting and planning. We decide to visit London, England, and Paris, France, and tour Ireland and Italy. Since the all-inclusive tours were out of our budgeted price range, we decided to plan the trip ourselves. I was in charge of accommodations, and he was in charge of transportation (to, between, and in each country).

I ended up tracking down and connecting with our relatives in Ireland and in Italy, who are the most kind and hospitable people in the world and offered to let us stay with them while we were in their respective countries.

Our first stop was London. We stayed in an awesome flat (picked by yours truly) not far out of the central part of the city and took the train or walked into town. It took me exactly two hours after we had settled into our Ikea display-esque two-bedroom flat to realize I hadn't properly calculated the number of batteries I would need to power my cochlear implant processor for the entire trip.

By my new calculations, I would be enjoying the last two days of our trip in complete silence. Oops. Of course, these batteries were insanely rare and impossible to find abroad. So on day one of our trip, I started turning off my processor whenever we were on the tube or in a museum (when I didn't need them to navigate complicated British accents that can't be lip-read easily) and forcing my brother to use what sign language he knew to communicate with me.

In London, we took the Tube everywhere. I loved the Tube! Unfortunately, I also had no sense of direction; my brother was the navigator, making sure we got where we needed to go. We only had a couple days, so we rushed to see Big Ben, Westminster Abbey, Parliament, the Tower of London, and a bunch of other tourist attractions.

They just loved audio tours! Every attraction had an audio tour option. While I walked through Westminster Abbey imagining the cold stone faces that guarded the tombs of Britain's royalty come to life, I was feeling the echoes of people's shoes on the stone floors bounce off the expansive room in silence.

My brother listened to the history behind each name that was chiseled in those walls and repeated them for me after we left. This became our system. I walked through historic sites imagining them in their former glory, and he relayed random facts to me from the audio guides he carried.

We got to see a lot in the short amount of time we had. The only thing we didn't get to do (that I regret to this day) is take the Harry Potter tour. (Just because I am in a different country doesn't mean my geekiness gets suppressed). From London, we headed to Ireland.

*Andrew and Amanda visiting
London, England, and
standing in front of Big Ben.*

At the airport, we were greeted by our two cousins, Steve and his wife, Breda, who had selflessly put their lives on hold to show us around Ireland during our stay. They were Walshes, related to my brother and I through my mom's Irish side (her grandfather).

Steve is the unofficial keeper of the family history and wanted to make sure we had the opportunity to learn where we came from. Steve and Breda drove us along the rolling green Irish countryside, stopping occasionally to ask directions from strangers and apologize for not having any room in their vehicle every time they saw a hitchhiker. My brother and I were in awe.

One only hitchhikes or stops to talk to a hitchhiker in LA if one has a death wish or is an Uber driver. Our cousins had to explain to us that, in Ireland, people aren't generally psychotic killers like they are in Los Angeles and that they regularly, safely have conversations with strangers on the side of the road. This was a shocking revelation for the two young Americans in their backseat.

During our Irish road trip, our cousins introduced us to the Irish breakfast—something I found to be superior to the "American breakfast" in every way. Fresh cooked meats, potatoes, eggs, sausages, and vegetables (that I am pretty sure didn't contain massive amounts of growth hormones and pesticides) graced our plates every morning and made our mouths water!

We visited our family's historic farm and learned about our ancestors. We visited a war memorial on the field where our great-uncle had been shot in the ass by the British (true story). We even visited a museum in Cork, the West Cork Heritage Center, that had shelves lined with artifacts bearing our family name, Walsh.

It turns out our ancestors did one of the most noble things you can do as an Irishman back in the day—they made alcohol. My brother and I were mesmerized with the family history and soaked up as much as Steve would share with us. Before we left the museum, the curator (a man who looked like he had seen close to a hundred winters) smiled at me, and with his incredibly thick accent, ushered me over to a smaller display case.

He pulled out a small well-preserved bottle that read "Little Norah." It was a quinine tonic, which still contained its original liquid contents, with an illustration of a young woman in a red hood on the bottle. He explained to me that the young woman on its face was modeled after one of my direct ancestors.

The bottle was old, but as I studied the sketched face on the front of the small bottle, I saw some features that I recognized from my own face. The curator looked at me and said, "I thought you looked familiar." He handed me the bottle and told me to keep it. He literally gave me a one hundred-year-old piece of my family's history with my ancestor's face on it to keep!

I was in shock and confused. I thought I was misunderstanding or misreading his lips. Steve looked a little jealous, and Breda was giddy with excitement. I walked out of that old church, which now served as the museum, with the bottle in my hand, completely in awe of Irish hospitality and kindness.

We spent a few more days in Ireland drinking Guinness, eating great food, meeting more of our amazing Irish family members, and walking around Dublin with one of my expatriate friends from my Disneyland days. When the day came for us to leave, my brother and I felt like we were leaving a part of ourselves in Ireland with the extended family we had just met.

As our last action in Ireland, we wrapped the family artifact, wrote thank you letters, and gifted it to Steve, our family historian whose kindness and hospitality knew no bounds. That bottle of Little Norah had inspired me and made me feel in touch with my family history, but now it belonged with him.

The Little Norah bottle being held in front of the museum in Ireland where it was given as a gift to Amanda.

Our next stop was Paris, France. There, people kept mistaking my brother and I for a couple—which grossed us both out to an appropriate degree. We watched the Eiffel Tower light up at dusk, walked the streets, and saw the sights. To be honest, I didn't love Paris like everyone had promised I would.

I did, however, fall in love with the Louvre. The day we planned to go to the Louvre, it closed early. When we arrived, we only had two hours to view one of the largest museums in the world! We entered in an art gallery filled with beautiful romantic paintings.

My brother likes to examine each painting and then translate the placard under it from French to English on his phone. This tried my patience in every museum we visited because I like to enjoy the atmosphere in its entirety. I would imagine myself as a queen in an elegant ornate baroque gown walking the halls as we toured palaces.

I would make up life stories for the serious people in the museum portraits labeled *Young Peasant Boy* or *Upper-Class Woman*. I would picture the statues coming to life and politely offering me fruit in the gardens. I was impatient to see as much as I possibly could in the very little time I had.

I ditched my brother, imagined I was in one of those *National Treasure* movies with Nicholas Cage and that there were clues hidden on various levels of the museum. I saw the Mona Lisa (she was smaller than I expected) surrounded by a mob of very rude Chinese tourists armed with selfie sticks and fanny packs.

It was nearly impossible to get to her. With my small stature, I can usually skillfully weave my ways through large crowds unnoticed, but getting to the middle of this herd was like escaping from Alcatraz (a swimming-like motion was actually used in the process).

I viewed artwork, mummies, rare china, statues, weapons, pottery, sarcophaguses, and so much more as I skipped, speed walked, and (for just a few moments) full-on ran. I even enjoyed a few moments of watching tourists look at paintings, feigning interest, and wondering how long they had to stare at the painting before they could move on so that no one would know that they had no idea what they are actually looking at.

I recognized theselooks well because I'd also made them at the very beginning of our European trip. In the two hours I spent there, before being escorted out of the atrium of statues of the building by a security guard who was very anxious to clock out and go home, I fell in love with the Louvre.

Paris had some great sights—the bridge full of locks, Notre Dame, the Moulin Rouge (which we stayed directly across the street from), and the Eiffel tower, to name a few, but nothing touched me as much as the Louvre. Someday, I will return and finish gathering clues on every floor for my *National Treasure* hunt. Who knows? Maybe I will bring the real-life Nicholas Cage with me next time, instead of just imagining he is there. Anything is possible.

The last country on our list was Italy. We started in Milan, where my brother, who is an amateur photographer, found one of his favorite cathedrals of the trip to photograph, and I pretended I was someone who could afford the beautiful designer clothes in the window displays.

Next, we took a train to Venice, Italy, my favorite of the Italian cities. Venice was a place where maps were useless because it was a city of bridges floating atop water, where every building was unique but also somehow all looked exactly the same when you needed to get somewhere.

The painted street names had long been weathered from the sides of the buildings, which existed like they were trapped in time somehow, in this perfect state of decay that is purely romantic in its undeniable beauty. The only way to navigate Venice is by remembering landmarks like turn left when you see the beautiful golden mask in the shop window, right at the restaurant with red flowers on the outdoor tables, and right again at the old church.

I excelled at navigating in Venice, where I had failed in every other city. Walking through these streets was like walking through history. I loved it! We rented an apartment during our stay and saved money on food by buying milk and cereal at the local grocers instead of spending fifteen to twenty-five euros each morning on breakfast.

I did still eat at least one margarita pizza a day at various restaurants around the island, though. We spent our days exploring. We crossed the Bridge of Sighs, soaked in the golden ceilings of St. Marks Basilica, navigated the canals, shopped for souvenirs, and walked through the Doge's Palace.

I was very reluctant to leave Venice when our time there ended. Something about the city made me feel free. But onto Florence we trekked. In Florence, we marveled at the beauty of the ceiling of the Duomo as we attended a Catholic Mass there, visited museums, saw David and other famous works of art, did some of our best shopping (aka a hilarious David statue cooking apron for our grandmother), and hiked to the top of a large hill to watch the sun set over the city.

We had been walking for six to thirteen miles a day for a couple weeks at this point, and it was starting to catch up with my feet, which were bruised, blistered, and bloody from overuse and improper shoe packing. The pain started slowing me down about halfway through our days. (If you ever travel Europe, forget the cute boots at home, and go full-on mom tennis shoe. Your feet will thank you).

From Florence, we headed to Rome, where we saw the Colosseum and took one of those Red Bus tours of the city (because we didn't have enough time there to explore it on our own).

Our father is a very devout Roman Catholic who rarely misses Sunday Mass at home. Being raised Roman Catholic, my brother and I found it important to visit Vatican City while we were nearby. It was a spiritual experience for both of us from the second we stepped off that bus and beheld the Vatican for the first time, with its round column-encircled courtyard reaching out to us as if to embrace us.

The courtyard was protected by statues atop the roof that wrapped partially around the courtyard, leaving an open welcoming space down its center. As we entered and moved toward the church, we felt their eyes on us. When we entered the church, my brother and I were both rendered speechless by the sheer size of it all.

We walked forward in awe, trying to take in the grandeur. It was perfect, exactly what it should be. At the end of a long walk down the church's center, there is an altar. Natural light from the heavens shines down upon it, making it the brightest thing in the gigantic room. It is an ethereal experience, which my brother and I will always cherish.

The next day my cousin Valeria and her father came to pick us up from our hotel and take us to their home, Castro Di Sangro, a small village tucked away peacefully in a small valley of the mountains a few hours outside of Rome near a breathtaking lake. You can't help but adore it the moment you see it for the first time.

It is picturesque, like something from a movie, with its cobblestone streets, ancient-looking church, and fountain in the center of town. After spending so much time touring crowded tourist attractions, it was a welcomed change.

There we ate gigantic homemade Italian meals, prepared for us by my cousin and her lovely mother. We sat at a small table together. My brother and I spoke no Italian, and my cousin's parents spoke no English, but communication flowed well (with a little help from my bilingual cousin Valeria).

In their two-bedroom home, in a small beautiful village, we felt safe and accepted. I also ate the best tiramisu of my life. I have tried dozens of tiramisu since and have not found one that even slightly measures up to the one my young cousin (she was around eighteen at the time) prepared for our stay. She even sent me the recipe, and

I have failed many times to replicate it. They took us on a beautiful tour of many amazing historic sites, but it was their village that left the strongest impression on me.

When it was time for my brother and I to say goodbye, it was hard. Valeria's father drove us to the Roman airport (which, like LAX, is a nightmare). We actually ended up missing our flight and having to pay for a new flight home the next day. We found this random church a few miles from the airport that let people rent beds in the basement for cheap; we rented two beds, took a taxi there, and spent the night.

The complex had beautiful, lush green grounds with peacocks roaming. It was in the middle of nowhere. There was no food for miles, just green pastures and lots of sheep. At 8:00 p.m., the church locked the gates, and we were locked in. It had a horror movie air about it. I may be Deaf, but I have never been in a quieter, more still environment than the one we experienced at that church.

There were no people to be found (except the man of few words who pensively manned the front desk until curfew). My brother and I actually agreed that we were pretty sure we were about to live out a horror film scenario. This was amazing because we never agree on anything and spent a good portion of the trip fighting like cats and dogs.

Obviously, we didn't die though. We used the last of our budgeted money to eat dinner with the priests who lived there—though it took us forever to find the dining room through the horror-esque maze of halls. After we ate, we hid in our simple basement room with two glorified cots the rest of the night. In the morning, we took a taxi back to the airport to go home. This trip got my mind off my troubles and helped my brother and I grow closer in the process.

17

THE IN-BETWEENER:
ONE FOOT IN DEAF CULTURE
AND ONE IN HEARING CULTURE

Doubting My Identity

No matter how hard I worked or how many electrodes my doctors were able to reactivate after that accident, I never was able to regain the access to sound with my implant that I'd had before the accident. I decided that losing my hearing three times in my life was just God's way of telling me that he'd made me to be Deaf.

Deafness was always his plan for me. Knowing that gave me some peace. Yet one of the things that surprised both my Deaf and hearing peers was that I never regretted getting my cochlear implant, despite how many struggles I have had with it. At the same time, I loved going days without it, in natural, peaceful silence.

I guess that "walking contradiction" thing doesn't just apply to my personality. I may have chosen to get the implant originally because I wanted to become more "hearing," but its meaning had changed for me as I finally figured out who I was.

Now, instead of it existing to try to make me into something I was not (a hearing person), the implant stood for access and inclusion. It gave me the power to be myself. It gave me the power to choose how I wanted to communicate at any given time. It eliminated some unnecessary limits from my life.

After returning to the states rejuvenated and with a new sense of self, I started searching for a part-time job to help me pay the bills as I finished recovering from the accident. Because I still wasn't able to utilize my implant at the same level as I could prior to the car accident and would need a little more assistance doing my job now, I felt it was only fair to be up front and honest and identified myself as Deaf on my applications.

After submitting dozens of job applications, I finally got an interview. I walked into the plain white interview room with a few obligatory propaganda posters on the wall glorifying the Fortune 500 company it belonged to. The interviewers had originally requested that I do my interview over the phone, but with my implant only partially working and not enough confidence in my sign language skills to do it over videophone with an interpreter, I asked for a face-to-face interview.

This request was denied a few times, but I was persistent. I had to fight tooth and nail for that face-to-face interview for a part-time, low-paying front desk job at a famous hotel. I even went down to the location and got a recommendation from the on-site managers e-mailed to the company's hiring department before they would grant their openly Deaf applicant an in-person job interview.

Once there, I was greeted by a strong woman with a short haircut wearing business casual. She gestured for me to take a seat. "You people normally bring an interpreter with you" was the first sentence out of her mouth when she noticed I had come alone.

The words *you people* felt like they were echoing in my head, but I shrugged it off and started talking about my qualifications, college education, and familiarity with her company. I mentioned that I came recommended by her current management team, but she was more interested in asking me a series of dozens of questions about how I was "able" to even hold the jobs listed on my résumé and how I was "able" to speak so well.

I answered her inquiries as politely as I could, not letting her know she was getting to me. Then, at the very end of the interview, she turned her chair around; faced away from me toward the white wall with a movie poster on it; and said, "Can you hear me now?" testing my hearing—the hearing of a candidate who had openly identified herself as Deaf on the job application.

I had no idea how to react to this kind of treatment. The last time I had interviewed for this same type of job after college and my second cochlear implant surgery, I had not openly disclosed my hearing loss, but none of these questions had been asked. The focus of that first interview was my work experience, and I had been hired quickly.

This time, I was put on a "waiting list" to see if the job that myself and several other people sitting in the waiting room were there to interview for would "open up in the near future." All of a sudden, during my interview, the job I was interviewing for "wasn't actually available."

Three months later, I received an e0-mail asking if I would like to remain on that "waiting list." I clicked "yes." Again, three more months later, I received the same e-mail, and again I clicked "yes." Then I never heard from the company again.

I wish I could say that this was an isolated incident, but it wasn't. I ended up going through several more interviews and had the same issues, all simply because I identify as "Deaf." Some people probably would have sued, but that's not my style.

It was tough identifying as a Deaf person sometimes. It wasn't just society's stereotypes and the limits the world, all of a sudden, was trying to force onto me. It was also difficult because of the rules the Deaf community was trying to get me to conform to. Many Deaf elitists wanted me to stop using my voice and utilize sign language only to be considered "deaf enough."

But that wasn't who I was. I had grown up in hearing culture. English was my first language. That was a part of who I was, just as much as being deaf was. A part of me would always want to be a part of the culture I grew up in—no matter how desperate I was to be accepted by this new Deaf culture that understood me.

I wanted to give myself my best chance for a successful future by being a part of both worlds. I decided not to stop using my voice but, instead, to encourage others to feel proud of theirs. Being able to speak is a beautiful skill, one that no one should ever be ashamed of. I also chose to continue studying sign language and to learn more about Deaf culture and history, which led to me discovering that it was a blessing to be involved in both cultures.

I never really felt like I 100 percent fit in with my Deaf peers. I also never felt like I fit 100 percent in with my hearing peers. But now that I felt like my feet were more firmly planted, and I had more of an acceptance and understanding of who I actually was, I started to think of myself as an "in-betweener."

This is a word I made up for a person with one foot in one culture and one in another culture. I stood there straddling the canyon between the two, hoping not to fall in and lose myself again. At the same time, I was kind of like a bridge. I helped my Deaf friends understand why hearing people did some of the things they did and vice versa for my hearing friends.

I decided that I liked feeling like I had the best of both worlds. I loved that I could sign with my Deaf friends, talk with my hearing friends, and sim-com (simultaneously communicate) when both were present at the same time. I had spent so much of my life unable to communicate and feeling left out that I decided I would never be the one to cause anyone else to feel that pain. I worked on all my forms of communication. I focused on being all-inclusive.

I didn't fit any stereotype. Even though I still used the word *Deaf* to describe myself in public (because "in-betweener" is a made up word that no one actually knows the meaning of), I didn't please everyone by acting the way anyone wanted me to. However, the more I accepted my in-betweener self, the more my confidence grew. The more my confidence grew, the more full my life started to feel.

18

FINDING MY PURPOSE: MAKING LIFE BETTER FOR PEOPLE WITH HEARING LOSS

YouTube Videos

The more Deaf and hard of hearing people I started to meet, the more I realized how many people out there felt as lost and ashamed and tortured as I had growing up. I realized that there were people struggling to live with hearing loss just like I had, and I felt the overwhelming need to help give them access to information that I wished I'd had access to when I was a kid.

I decided to use film, a medium that I was very comfortable with, to create videos with information in them for people going through what I had gone through and their friends and family members. I started with a video called 5 *Ways to Communicate with a Deaf Person*, which outlined five different communication methods for hearing people who don't know sign language to communicate with their Deaf or hard of hearing loved ones.

I bought a crappy camcorder online and a tripod and filmed it in my home. In the video, I decided to use sim-com (simultaneous communication), this is a form of communication where a person talks in English and simultaneously signs what he or she is saying. It is not sign language, because sign language has a different word order than English.

Now I knew my signing wasn't perfect. I was still learning. But I figured that people who were Deaf could read my hands, people who were hearing could listen to my words, and people who were hard of hearing could read my lips and the captions that I added to the video.

I uploaded the video to YouTube and my professional acting Facebook page. Before I knew it, the video had over twenty thousand views with lots of shares and comments. Most of the comments were positive and grateful for the information. A few criticized my use of sim-com, but the positive comments kept me going.

People thanked me for making them feel less alone and for providing them with information they could use in their daily lives. For those people, I kept making videos. I kept sharing what I learned as I learned it. I wasn't making any money on these videos. To my dad's dismay, the countless hours I spent filming, editing, and captioning them were never compensated. But the personal stories people shared with me about their own experiences with hearing loss were enough for me.

I loved sharing information that could help improve the lives of other, so I kept making videos as I grew and acquired more knowledge. I remained painfully aware that there were many things I still needed to learn and a lot of things I still needed to grow comfortable with as a Deaf person, though.

I started hoping for a day when I would stand up tall and not be afraid to ask for accommodations, like an interpreter on set for work. I pictured a day when I would feel comfortable using a video relay service to make important phone calls instead of asking for my mom's help.

I began visualizing a day when I knew the history of Deaf culture and Deaf people all around the world and could teach it to others—a day where mainstream culture understood my deafness and didn't limit me or pity me because of it and where Deaf culture understood my background and didn't criticize me for it.

I envisioned a day when I knew exactly who I was and what I wanted, and everyone (no matter what culture) understood and respected that.

Until that day came, I knew my outlook, my perspective, my chosen ways of communicating, and my opinions would probably change a half a million times, because I am human and capable of growth.

But until that day, I decided I would laugh off any haters and keep learning and striving to become the best version of me possible. I wanted to make this world better for people like me through art. One video became two and then three, and the information on my YouTube channel grew.

Acting

I made the YouTube videos to share information with others, but I still had a dream for myself—that one day I would be allowed to play any character, no matter what the character's abilities were. I wanted to work without bias, to be hired based on my acting skills, and to not be limited by other people's misconceptions about my "disability."

I started with the pilot turned web series *Just Us Guys* created by the talented writer Chris Lilly. This was my first audition for a principle Deaf role! I was excited to put the sign language and Deaf culture I had been learning from my fellow background actors on *Switched at Birth* to good use!

I felt pretty good about my first audition; it went well. I managed to get a callback, and I remember walking in and being the only girl there. I read with a few different male actors and was asked to stay to read with a few more. I ended up booking the pilot! I was so excited!

After filming *Just Us Guys*, I started booking other things—a short film called *Loud and Clear* in which I had a small role as the main character's Deaf best friend, a short student thriller named *Listen* in which I played the Deaf heroine in a horror story, and some other work.

After that, I worked on Dickie Heart's *Passengers*—a film made in forty-eight hours with a 100 percent Deaf cast and crew that has gone on to show in many film festivals and win awards. I am particularly proud of this film, even though my role was a small one, simply because it has broken down so many barriers in the film festival circuit.

Every festival we went to, we were the first Deaf people most of those filmmakers had ever met. Our film was the first time many of those filmmakers were exposed to the idea of a Deaf actor and sign language, and we were the ones teaching the festival coordinators how to work with a sign language interpreter to grant communication access to the Deaf.

From there, I booked more shorts (including *Silent Star, Complex Wine, De'Via, Pickles, Love Wins, Lady Electric,* and *The Love Project*) and worked on more independent projects within the Deaf community. I even booked myself and my friend print work for Google. We were given the opportunity to be photographed by world-famous photographer Andrew Southam for a Google Impact campaign. After that, I booked a national 7 Up campaign called *Music Lifts You Up.* This gave me the opportunity to work with Martin Garrix, a famous EDM DJ, and the 7 Up crew.

They built a dance club specifically for the Deaf. The engineers made the floor move to the beat, the speakers bounced with the bass, water danced with the vibrations, and we got to wear backpacks that had additional little speakers in them so that we could feel the beat. I literally got paid to have fun and dance the night away. It was a unique filming experience!

*A behind-the-scenes photo of
Amanda getting her hair and
makeup done on the set of her
national 7 Up commercial.*

I felt blessed to be working, yet I started to feel like I was being typecast. I missed the challenge of playing a hearing person. I loved creating those reactions to sound with my body, even when I couldn't actually hear the sound being created. I loved coming up with unique ways to get my cues, like using reflections in objects to see when an actor entered a room; feeling vibrations of movement through the floor; or even using actions, blocking, and reactions of the other actors present.

Playing a hearing character is like composing a symphony of vibrations, cues, and tricks to create the perfect reactions even when you lack the sound. I went ahead and wrote, produced, and filmed two short films where I play a hearing protagonist—*The Hunt* and *Two Girls in a Bar*—to show my agents and the world how completely naturally I could play multiple characters who possessed the ability to hear. Having these clips strengthened my demo reel, but I found that Casting Directors still had a hard time getting past that word *deaf* to see the actress I actually was. Getting these roles I longed for and convincing Casting Directors to take a chance on me, despite my "disability," became my newest challenge.

With great difficulty I began making a name for myself as an "actress who happens to be Deaf" instead of a "Deaf actress." I spent two hours a day submitting myself for roles, built my own website, maintained an actress physique, and took classes to practice my craft.

Then I booked my first network job since quitting my marketing work. My agent helped me get a costar role on NBC's *Bad Judge* starring Kate Walsh. I was to play an ASL interpreter, and I couldn't have been happier. This character was going to give me the opportunity to show off my English and sign language skills and show my agent and the community that I could pull off hearing roles and didn't have to be limited to only Deaf roles.

It was an amazing episode called "Communication Breakdown." It was all about barriers in communication.

In the episode, a Deaf man is on trial, but the court doesn't realize he is Deaf at first, so they try communicating with him in English and fail. Then they bring in an American Sign Language interpreter (played by me) to communicate with him, only to discover he doesn't know American Sign Language but, rather, Chinese Sign Language. So they bring in a Chinese Sign Language interpreter (played by a Deaf Chinese man) who didn't speak English. This then requires translation from Mandarin into English by yet another interpreter.

It was a brilliant script that had a great comedic approach to talking about communication barriers. Two of the actors playing interpreters, myself and Xiabo Song (the self-proclaimed Chinese Marlee Matlin) were both Deaf, and we had our own ASL interpreter on set to help us communicate behind the scenes.

There was also a bilingual actress on set who spoke Mandarin and English playing the third interpreter. Because Xiabo's English and American Sign Language were limited, we communicated with him partly through sign language and partly through Chinese character writing. Our little group of bilinguals had a running joke that day on set—"we use no less than two languages to communicate at any given time."

Amanda in front of her trailer
on the set of NBC's Bad Judge.

Soon after I came across a woman named Heyjin Jun. She was a student at USC's School of Cinematic Arts, and she was looking for a subject for her latest documentary. She found my story fascinating—much like Brian had when he'd created his radio broadcast story on my cochlear implant experience for KCRW two years earlier.

She wanted to tell my story differently though. She wanted to focus on my struggle as an actress who became Deaf and how my hearing loss had affected my performing career. She cut together footage from my childhood of me performing, dancing, and singing. She showed my transition into deafness and even footage from the moment my cochlear implant was turned on.

All of this led to this beautiful shot of me hiking up to the top of a steep hill and a narration about overcoming any obstacle and believing in yourself. It was beautiful, visual, and touching. There wasn't a dry eye in the theater during its premier.

I sat there watching it for the first time, surrounded by strangers and family in that USC movie theater, and I realized that there was power in talking about my personal struggle—the power to help others, to inspire others to improve their own lives, and to comfort others by making them realize that they are not alone.

Then it finally happened. My agents sent me an e-mail letting me know that the producers of *Switched at Birth* wanted to give me an opportunity to audition for a costar role on the show—the role of a young college student named Jenna. Finally, I would have the opportunity to show them that I was more than just a background actress!

I went in and auditioned and booked the role! I was psyched. The night of filming as I walked onto set, after going through wardrobe, hair, and makeup, members of the crew were coming up and patting me on the back. They congratulated me, saying, "It's about time."

This was the final season of the show, and I felt just like I had in high school with *Annie*, like God was giving me closure to complete this awesome chapter of my life. I owed so much of who I had become to that show and the amazing people who worked on it. It was nice to graduate from the background and finally have a name, even for just one scene.

A behind-the-scenes picture of Amanda on the monitor as she performed her scene as Jenna on ABC Family's Switched at Birth.

NYC

Around this same time, my brilliant mother wrote a book called *How to Make your Credit Score Soar*. She was tired of seeing people's bad credit scores stand in their way of homeownership. So she did something about it. She wrote a book to teach people how to improve their credit and how to find and dispute errors on their credit reports and explained in simple terms what credit scores are and how they affect us.

After she wrote the book, she was invited to attend a publicity conference in New York City. At this conference, members of the media would be present to listen to pitches from authors for articles, TV show segments, and radio interviews. Producers from *The View*, *The Today*

Show, 48Hours, Live with Kelly and Michael, and *The New York Times* to independent radio hosts on Sirius XM were there.

It was a wonderful opportunity for her to share her knowledge with a broader audience. She decided to bring me with her. She saw that I was still struggling, and she hoped that something in New York City would inspire me.

She was right. The streets of New York were alive. People hurried from one location to their destination, and they dressed to impress. The buildings all reached past the clouds. Bright billboards adorned with even brighter stars covered every inch of Times Square.

One of those billboards even displayed the faces of some dear friends from Deaf West's (a theater group that combined Deaf and hearing cultures) *Spring Awakening.* The play was so well received in LA that it was now playing right there on Broadway. Knowing that there was a group of young Deaf theater performers making their mark on the world in the Big Apple and that I just happened to be friends with them was elating. This trip couldn't have been more exciting for me. The whole city just swelled with possibilities.

We had rented an apartment through Airbnb for the week, just a few blocks from the conference, and it quickly became our home away from home. During the days, I was my mother's dutiful assistant. I carried stacks of her books and press releases, helping her customize each one of her pitches to speak to each media member's target audience and meeting with authors, writers, reporters, and producers. At night, we saw the city.

We walked through Times Square, sang "It's the Hard Knock Life" in front of the Chrysler building, danced on the street in front of the Radio City Music Hall, strolled through Central Park eating soft pretzels and window-shopped on Fifth Avenue. We even bought tickets to see my friends perform in *Spring Awakening* on Broadway. It was a breathtaking performance that blended sign language, a brilliant script, and music.

On the last day of the conference, my mother finished her pitches early. There were two men sitting on the far wall of the conference room together. They weren't members of the media. Rather, they were fairly well-known publishers. My mother turned her attention to them.

She walked over, with me in tow; strategically balancing stacks of books and papers; opened her mouth; and started telling these two strangers my life story. She talked about my hearing loss. She talked about me teaching myself to talk and lip-read. She talked about my graduation from college, as if I was some kind of superhero.

It was the first time I realized how incredibly proud my mother was of me. It took me a few seconds to realize she was pitching a book that would be written by *me*, about *my* life. I jumped in near the middle and began wrapping up the pitch myself. The two men were shocked I could even speak after hearing all of this about a "deaf girl."

When I finished my pitch, the two men said, "You need to write this book."

I didn't understand. "But who would even want to read a book about *me*?" I asked.

They smiled knowingly. My mother smiled at me, and in that moment, I knew I had a message that was ready to be heard.

19

THE HEARING-LOSS HANDBOOK

Losing your hearing is normal. Yes, I actually just wrote that. Hearing loss happens everywhere. People worldwide experience hearing loss. According to the World Health Organization, "360 million people worldwide have disabling hearing loss." That is roughly 5 percent of the world's population.

Nearly fifty million Americans experience hearing loss, according to the Hearing Health Foundation. Sure, losing one's hearing the way I did is not the social norm, but nearly everyone experiences some degree of hearing loss over the course of a lifetime.

Whether it is from old age, working with loud machinery, playing music too loud, suffering through an ear infection, attending a few too many concerts, genetics, illness, or the long-term use of certain prescription drugs, everyone eventually experiences some hearing loss. So why hasn't society acknowledged that this is a norm? In my opinion, it's because society is afraid.

There are thousands of different languages being used on this planet. Most of us speak at least one, many of us two, and the particularly talented know three or more. When people think of communication, when they think of language, they typically think of verbal exchanges. The thought of being deprived of sound, deprived of verbal communication, is terrifying. We are social creatures.

Communication allows us to share experiences, laughs, joy, disappointment, and anger. Most people simply don't realize that there isn't only one way to communicate. This idea of becoming unable to express thoughts, ideas, and feelings in the one way that we are comfortable with and that society tells us is "normal" is scary.

Most able-bodied people don't acknowledge sign language as a real language. Nor do they realize how much communicating they actually do nonverbally despite whatever words they are forming with their mouth. There is a fear of the unknown.

Every night when I was little, I would lie down in bed and pray to God that, when I woke up in the morning, I would have the same amount of hearing as I had gone to bed with. Each night, I closed my little eyes and held together my little hands and prayed as hard as I could. "Please don't let it get any worse, please, please, please."

Some days, I would wake up and know immediately that the sounds around me were different, that something was missing; other times, I would make it through half a day not realizing I could no longer hear the sound of the school bell.

Growing up, I was lucky to have parents who were financially stable. Had they not been, I would not have had access to the tools I needed to get through school and have a seminormal childhood. Hearing aids, goodness I hated them. I avoided wearing them as often as I could and even went through phases of refusing to wear them. When asked why, I would say that it was because they weren't "normal." Kids wearing glasses to see the board in class, that was *normal*, but hearing aids to hear the information the teacher was providing us was *weird*. If I hadn't hid them under my long hair my entire life, I am pretty sure I would have been bullied plenty.

I was ashamed of them. I was ashamed of me. They were a constant physical reminder that I was different, that I was missing something; but they shouldn't have been. Needing hearing aids is just as normal as needing glasses. A sense has decreased, and you are using a device that helps you get through your everyday life. There should be no shame in that. It is normal.

Believe it or not, there are even perks to having hearing loss. Among them is community. You don't have to be fully deaf to get support from the Deaf community. They are a great resource to learn new ways to communicate and get support from people who understand what life with hearing loss is like.

Another is technology. Now there is so much technology to help you communicate that it makes life a lot easier. Between text messages, e-mail, FaceTime, Skype, and video relay services, it has never been easier to communicate without sound.

Lastly, there's language. Sign language is a great way to communicate, and now it is easily accessible through the Internet and free classes. So grab a family member and start learning together!

Help us hear you: How to help the hard of hearing people in your life

1. **Eye contact** – Look at us when you speak. We need to see your lips, your body language, and your facial expressions to fully understand you.

2. **Speak normally** – Do not yell or exaggerate. Yelling or exaggerating your speech actually makes it harder for us to understand you. Talk like you normally would. We will tell you if we don't understand you and have you type up what you were saying or write it down.

3. **Reduce background noise** – Turn down or off any unnecessary noises (for example TV or radio) when you are trying to communicate with us. It allows us to utilize whatever hearing we do have, and it helps us focus our attention on you with fewer distractions.

4. **Use adjectives** – If we can't lip-read a word by the second repeat, use adjectives or examples. For example, if you are talking about the United States, but we aren't understanding "US," say, "America" or "the United States of America" to clarify. Another example would be, instead of repeating "Porsche" for the fifth time, start describing the car—its color, design, or origins—to help us understand what you are talking about.

5. **Communicate visually** – Write the information down, type it into a text, or show us pictures or videos on your phone—whatever it takes to help us understand you.

6. **Inclusion** – Make us feel included in the conversation by always facing us, letting us know when the subject has changed, and arranging the group in a circle if possible so we can see everyone's lips. It also helps a lot if you try your best not to speak over one another.

7. **Captions** – Turn on the captioning if we are watching TV or a movie with you. This way, we have access to the entertainment as well.

8. **Patience** – Be patient with us. Never say, "Never mind," or brush us off because you don't want to repeat yourself. Always take the time to try to communicate with us because we are taking our time to try to communicate with you.

9. **Be creative** – If we are struggling with one way of communicating, try a different way (writing, texting, ASL, lip-reading, to name a few examples). Don't give up. Get creative.

10. **Learn sign language** – This will always be the easiest way for Deaf or hard of hearing people to communicate. Learning sign language shows the Deaf or hard of hearing person in your life that you care enough to make sure you can always communicate with him or her.

Commonly Asked Questions

Imagine you are going about your day, minding your own business when a stranger walks up to you and asks you to do a triple blackflip. Can you do a triple backflip? No. Would it be cool if you could do a triple backflip? Absolutely! But can you go about your life perfectly happy having never done a triple backflip? Yes.

After explaining to this stranger that, unfortunately, you cannot complete a triple backflip for his enjoyment, he begins grilling you with questions like, "Why can't you do one? I can, I thought everyone could. What happened to you? It must be a very tragic story of how you have never been able to do one. Is your life really boring since you can't do a triple backflip? I'll pray for you. Do you ever watch people do triple backflips and wish you could too? How do you walk if you can't do a triple backflip? How do you work? Is your life terrible? I bet it is terrible. I feel so bad for you. My friend's sister's cousin's uncle's distant relative once knew someone who couldn't do a triple backflip, so I 100 percent understand what your life must be like."

Yes, I am aware of how ridiculous that last paragraph reads, but believe it or not, I get asked every single one of those questions and hear every single one of those comments on a daily basis. The only difference is that hearing is the action in question rather than performing triple backflips (which, for the record, I can't do either).

Let's just get one thing straight right off the bat: *Not all deaf people have zero hearing.* Yes, you read that correctly. You see, there are various levels of hearing loss—mild, moderate, severe, and profound hearing loss. I personally have no natural hearing left at all. I am "profoundly deaf."

However, that is not the case for most of my Deaf/deaf and hard of hearing friends. Most of them can listen to music, hear sounds like sirens, and hear people talking (though their understanding of speech is usually minimal). Some can even talk on the phone.

There is this misconception that all Deaf people live in complete silence, which is simply not true. Even I am able to hear something with the help of a device called a cochlear implant when I have it turned on. Here are my reactions to a few of the questions I mentioned above but with regards to hearing loss instead of triple backflips.

"I'll pray for you." Well, that is a lovely notion, but my hearing isn't magically coming back overnight. I am a Christian, and I think it is wonderful to pray for one another, but being Deaf is part of my identity. Saying you would pray for God to change who I am and how I identify myself can be hurtful.

However, I would gladly accept prayers for my health, family, a cure for cancer, world peace, an end to poverty, free education for all humans, an end to terrorism, or a solution to our escalating national debt. Being Deaf is part of who I am; it isn't something I would even want to change if I could.

"Can you drive?" Yes, I can drive! Not all deaf or hard of hearing choose to drive, but it is 100 percent legal for us to hold drivers licenses. After all, we can see the road, use mirrors, check for blind spots, use the pedals, and turn the steering wheel without needing to use our ears. People often follow up that question with, "But how do you hear emergency vehicles then?"

The answer is I don't need to; I see them. Deaf people are very aware of their surroundings. I usually see the emergency vehicle before hearing people start reacting to it. If I don't, the chaos and confusion that happens when hearing drivers do start hearing a faraway siren alerts me to the presence of an oncoming emergency vehicle. I simply safely pull over to the side of the road and wait for it to pass. See, it's not rocket science; one just has to be aware and observant of their surroundings.

"I'm sorry." I'm not. Becoming Deaf was the best thing that ever happened to me. When I lost the last of my hearing, I had to admit that I was different. That acceptance changed my life. For the first time in my life, I got to be myself, instead of pretending I was someone else, instead of pretending I could hear or hiding from new situations. Deafness gave me freedom, and I will never be sorry for that. I am Deaf and proud like so many others in Deaf culture, so please don't belittle my situation by apologizing for it. I'm not sorry.

"But you talk so well. You can't be Deaf." Newsflash, my ears don't work, but my vocal cords are fine. I know you are trying to compliment me, but it is kind of a backhanded compliment anytime someone is surprised I can do something. I can do anything, except hear without my processor on.

Please don't embarrass me by pointing out my speech. Though it is true some Deaf people do not talk at all and many of us have "deaf speech" or an accent, please don't point it out. Usually there is a long history of struggles, speech therapy, and difficulties behind what hearing people consider "good speech."

Yes, it is a great accomplishment to be able to speak well. It took me years of daily practice, and it is embarrassing to have it pointed out every time we meet a new person who does not know sign language.

"Since you are Deaf, you know sign language right?" You don't become deaf and magically know sign language or opt to just download it into your brain. Just like with all languages, you must learn sign language, word by word, and it takes years to become fluent.

I have been signing since 2013 and still don't feel confident in my translations all the time. Just because someone is deaf doesn't mean they can sign. Most deaf and hard of hearing kids are actually born into hearing families, and very few of those families make an effort to learn sign language. Many of us who have been deaf most of our lives were not exposed to sign language and, therefore, did not learn to communicate that way.

"Your life must be so terrible." It's not. My life is actually kind of awesome. I do everything hearing people do—hang out with friends, watch movies, eat, go dancing, complain about bad first dates, date some more, play mini golf, swim, bowl, travel, attend concerts. You name it, and Deaf people can do it.

"How can you enjoy music if you can't hear?" Music is vibrations. Even when my processor is off and I can't hear any sound, I can still feel the music. Literally. I'm actually not a terrible dancer, and I even sing better than my tone-deaf cousins. Not only can I enjoy music, I can make it.

"If you can talk, why don't you just talk all the time?" Why don't you use sign language all the time? Talking is hard, especially when I am without my processor. I can't gauge my volume. Sometimes my words get jumbled, or I trip up during sentences. It is much more difficult producing sound when you can't hear it than people give us credit for.

Some days, I prefer to write on paper or type on my phone what I would say to someone else. It's not because I hate talking but because it can be frustrating, difficult, and sometimes embarrassing. Just please respect my decision to communicate with you in whatever way I feel comfortable doing so at that moment, whether it be talking, typing, texting, signing, or using an interpreter.

"Can you tell her what I am saying?" (Talking to my interpreter, instead of just talking to me). I'm not invisible so please don't treat me like I am. My interpreter is there to help me communicate, not to create a wall between me and those around me. Look at me when you talk. The interpreter won't be insulted. It is part of his or her job. Look me in the eye when you ask me a question.

Let me feel like I am actually connecting with you, rather than making me feel different or separate. If you want to ask my name and my interpreter is standing right next to me, walk right up, look at me, and ask me my name. I won't bite. I promise.

"Can you read my lips?" Yes. How else did you think I was able to understand you during the first five minutes of this conversation? Mind reading? Although that would be very cool, I can't read minds. If you know sign language, that is my preferred style of communication. But if you don't, I will read your lips or ask you to write down or type up what you are saying.

Just don't yell or exaggerate your words. Be yourself, talk like you would normally, and look at me when you talk. If I don't understand you, I will let you know. (Note: Not all Deaf people can read lips, so don't ever assume we can. Be prepared with a paper or your phone to type up information).

"If you have a cochlear implant, then why aren't you wearing it?" Cochlear implants are a great tool for those of us with profound hearing loss, like hearing aids are for those with a bit more hearing left. However, they are not comfortable. Nor are they practical to wear all the time.

They fall off when you work out, play sports, or are doing many other types of activity. They aren't waterproof, so I don't even wear mine if I know I will be around water. Also, sometimes I just want to feel comfortable and natural and enjoy the silence of being Deaf.

"You have a cochlear implant? That means you are not Deaf anymore right?" Wrong. A cochlear implant is merely a tool. It helps me hear when it is turned on but returns me to a life of silence when it comes off or runs out of battery. A cochlear implant is no more than an advanced hearing aid for those of us who can no longer be assisted by hearing aids. I am and forever will be Deaf.

Things to do when interacting with a Deaf person

1. **Ask how we prefer to communicate.** This will save you both time and any possible awkwardness. Some Deaf people read lips, but not all do. Some will prefer you type your words into a phone or write them on a piece of paper. They may even wave down an interpreter to facilitate more fluid communication. (Note: When using an interpreter, always talk to the Deaf person. The interpreter is just a facilitator for communication. He or she is not who you are communicating with.)

2. **Treat us like a normal human being** because we are normal human beings. We listen to music, eat food, date, have our hearts broken, and fight with our siblings just like you do. Keep that in mind.

3. **Please be respectful of our language and culture.** We don't expect you to magically know all of our cultural norms, but if we ask you to use the identifiers *Deaf* or *hard of hearing* to describe us instead of *hearing impaired*, simply respect our wishes.

4. **Show an interest in communicating with us.** If you start a conversation with a Deaf or hard of hearing person, and the person lets you know that he or she is Deaf or hard of hearing, don't walk away. Make an effort to continue the conversation with us, using our preferred method of communication, just like you would if we were hearing.

5. **Face us when speaking in a group setting** to make sure we can still see your lips. This is something so simple that can make us feel accepted and included in the conversation.

6. **Set chairs up in a circle** (at dinner or meetings) so we can see everyone who will be speaking clearly. If there are any centerpieces or other objects that could obstruct our view, simply remove them from the table.

7. **Let us know when you change the subject** in a group conversation. If we look lost, it usually is because we are. If the subject changes in a group conversation, take a few seconds to let us know. It helps us a lot to know the general context of what people are talking about.

8. **Write down or finger spell names or places if we don't understand** them the first time. If we have you repeat a name multiple times, then pull out your phone and type the name for us to see, or write it on a piece of paper. You get bonus points if you are able to finger spell the name.

10 Things not to do around a Deaf person

1. **Exaggerate your speech.** It makes lip-reading more difficult. Just speak normally. If we can't understand you, we will let you know.

2. **Yell.** We still can't hear you. Now you just look ridiculous to the other hearing people in the room.

3. **Fake sign/hand gestures.** It is like making up fake Chinese words by making random sounds to a native Chinese person. Don't do it.

4. **Say, "Never mind."** Brushing us off by refusing to repeat yourself and saying, "Never mind," is hurtful. It shows us that you don't care enough to even try to communicate with us.

5. **Test our lipreading skills.** Lipreading is not a parlor trick. We do not do it for other people's amusement. We lip-read to communicate and survive. So, please do not "test" our lipreading skills with silly words like *watermelon* or asking us what that guy across the room is saying. We don't find it funny.

6. **Look at the interpreter and ignore the Deaf person.** If a sign language interpreter is present in your conversation, pretend the interpreter is invisible and focus 100 percent of your attention in the Deaf or hard of hearing person you are talking to. Imagine the interpreter's voice is actually coming from the Deaf person. This is a common mistake people make. They talk to the interpreter, asking things like, "Can she understand me?" or, "Can you ask her if she wants to come to the event on Saturday?" Instead, direct your questions to the person you are actually talking to. For example, "Can you come to the event this Saturday?"

7. **Tell us you feel bad for us for being Deaf or hard of hearing.** People who identify as Deaf or hard of hearing tend to be very proud people. Pride in our identity is part of our

culture. We see ourselves as just as able as our hearing peers. These statements imply that being Deaf or hard of hearing is a negative thing that makes us less than our hearing peers, which just isn't true.

8. **Comment on how good or bad our speaking abilities are.** This is a personal pet peeve of mine. I know oftentimes people mean it as a compliment, but, "Wow, you speak so well for a Deaf person," feels to me like, "Wow, I had really low expectations or your ability to speak based on inaccurate media portrayals of Deaf people that I have now imposed on you, so I am going to compliment you on it."

9. **Call us *hearing impaired*.** It is an outdated title, just like *deaf and dumb* is outdated. *Hearing impaired* has a negative connotation and is felt to be offensive to the Deaf community. Instead, use the terms *deaf* or *hard of hearing.*

10. **Leave us out of a group conversation.** It is just rude. Even though it might take a few extra steps, always include us.

Ways to Communicate with a Deaf Person

People are usually too shy or afraid of offending me to ask me what they can do to make communication with me easier. I wish they would; it comes down to just a few things:

Look at me when you talk. This makes it easier for me to read your lips. It's also polite. If you look away in the middle of a sentence, and I can't get a clear view of the movement of your lips, I am not going to understand you, no matter how talented I am at lipreading.

Talk normally. Don't overexaggerate your speech and don't yell. Neither of those things is going to help me understand you. Plus, they are both superunattractive.

If lipreading isn't working, don't give up on communicating with me. Just change methods.

Write it down. Take out a piece of paper and write down what you want me to know. I'll be able to read the information and write back to you—well as long as your handwriting is better than my dad's.

Text it out on your phone. Everyone has a cell phone these days, so use it! Open a new text message or notes document and text out what you want to say to me. You can even be superlazy nowadays and just say what you want into your phone and have your phone do the typing for you. Ta-da, communication.

Type it up. If you are wondering the best way to get in touch with me after we meet, here is a clue: Phone calls are not my thing. E-mail is much more efficient for me. Plus, it has the added bonus of allowing me to go back and review the information you provided me at a later date. So type it out!

Sign it. Yes I am aware that not everyone knows sign language, but if you do, even a little, use it! If you don't, learn a few signs like "yes," "no," "thank you," or "you're welcome" to help make the next Deaf person you bump into feel accepted. Plus, it is fun.

Interpret it. There are these amazing and talented people out there who interpret between the Deaf and hearing for a living. They know sign language and English and use their knowledge to help bridge the gap between the two worlds. If you are using this method, you will need to grab the nearest interpreter and ask him or to help you or hire an interpreter to assist you.

One really important thing to remember is that the interpreter is just the voice of the Deaf person, not the actual person you are communicating with. Make sure to look at the Deaf person when you talk, not the interpreter. That is kind of a Deafie pet peeve.

Lastly, **never give up**. Try as many methods as it takes to communicate with me or any other Deaf person. Use your resources to explain yourself.

Show us videos, pictures, web pages, or whatever you have at your disposal to help us understand what you are trying to convey.

Never say, "Never mind," or just drop the topic. That makes us feel isolated and not worth your time. It is rude and hurtful. So get out there, get creative, and talk to a Deaf person!

Common communication challenges

1. **Facial Hair.** Facial hair has a tendency to cover lips, making it more difficult for the Deaf and hard of hearing to communicate with you. If you have someone Deaf or hard of hearing in your life, you may need to either shave the beard or mustache off, keep it very well groomed to provide maximum lip visibility, or learn sign language so that the person never need to read your lips.

2. **Accents.** Strong accents can make it a little more difficult for us to understand a person. Having an accent is not the person's fault; nor is it something they can really change. It just takes a little more patience for us to communicate with people with accents, and we may need to have them repeat themselves many times or use writing, typing, or signing to assist in communicating with us.

3. **Dim lighting** is the arch nemesis of the Deaf and hard of hearing. It prevents clear communication either through lipreading or sign language. When picking a restaurant to eat at or an event to attend, keep the lighting in mind.

4. **Loud atmosphere noise or music** is incredibly distracting for people with hearing loss. It prevents us from being able to utilize the hearing we do have. Turn down the music on the car ride if you want to have a conversation or pick a restaurant that isn't noisy if you want to go out to eat. The only place for loud music

is concerts, clubs, or live band performances, and we tend to love all of those. (They also tend to be great places for utilizing sign language. Just saying.)

Tips for Learning American Sign Language

1. **Learn from free classes, online resources, apps, or community college.** Many community colleges offer sign language classes. There are also some free classes offered at local churches or community centers, depending on where you live. There are lots of online resources like YouTube, Facebook, Handspeak.com, ASLPro.com, and others to help you practice and improve your signing skills. Also, there are many sign language apps you can simply download on your phone now to increase your vocabulary on the go. Most of these can be found with a simple Google search or by asking around your community.

2. **Learn with a partner.** Keep each other motivated and practice together! It helps a lot to have conversations in the language you're learning with others. It is not all about being able to do the signs, you have to be able to see and understand them as well.

3. **Learn to sign songs and keep it fun.** Songs are a great, entertaining way to learn some new signs. Print out the lyrics and start translating your song using an online sign language dictionary as a resource. Or learn other sign language user's translations on YouTube!

4. **Practice by watching ASL YouTube videos** and seeing how much you understand. Turn the closed captions off and watch videos that are in sign language only. You may not understand it all the first time. Just rewind and rewatch the parts you struggle with till you understand them. Then you can check

your work by turning the captioning on and watching it all the way through.

5. **Find your Resources.** There are some great web resources like ASLpro.com, Handspeak.com, DPAN TV, and some great YouTube channels to help assist your learning. Do a search and explore them to see which work best for you and your learning style. There are also some wonderful books available to assist you in your sign language learning journey on Amazon. There are also many Deaf events and meet-ups where you can practice and learn ASL from fluent people who are members of the Deaf community. These events vary by location and can often be found through Facebook event searches. They are usually open to anyone at any level of skill in sign language. Check for any specifics or restrictions.

Workplace Changes to make Life Easier with Hearing Loss

1. **Request e-mails instead of phone calls.** This way you can read information instead of struggling to hear it.

2. **Do videoconferencing instead of phone conferencing.** Videoconferencing, like Skype, allows you to see your business associate, which gives you a lot more information about the person's mood and tone and allows you to see his or her lips. Note: You can also request an interpreter or captioner to assist you during the videoconference call.

3. **Request interpreters or real-time captioners** ahead of time for company meetings and events to help you keep up with what is being said. Although many people with hearing loss do okay in one-on-one conversations, group conversations are usually not accessible. Having an interpreter or real-time captioner present allows you access to all the information being said.

4. **Find ways to make your work place hearing-loss friendly.** Ask to get a desk that faces out toward the office. This allows you to see people approaching you from the front, rather than having them pop up behind you. This way, you can be prepared for the conversation before it happens instead of being caught off guard. If the office is dimly lit, making it difficult for you to see people's lips or signs, request brighter bulbs be put in the office to improve the lighting. These are just a few examples. Every work environment is different, so you will have to come up with accommodations specific to yours. Just make sure you are comfortable and can produce your best work in the environment.

5. **Learn your rights.** The Americans with Disabilities Act guarantees employees the right to "reasonable accommodations" in the workplace. Know your rights and think of accommodations to ask for in advance for the things you know will be more difficult for you. It is important to know your rights so that no employer can deny you reasonable accommodations at work.

Tips for Making School More Accessible When You Have Hearing Loss

1. **Find out what services your school offers.** Most colleges have a Disability Resource Center that can provide this information for you. Other schools often have counselors who can help you find out what services you could benefit from.

2. **Request interpreters or captioners in your classes.** If you are fluent in sign language, having an interpreter in your classes will ensure you don't miss any of the material. If you are not fluent in sign language, you can request a real-time captioner in your classes. Captioners type up what is being said in real time, and you simply read the information off a

laptop in front of you to make sure you don't fall behind or miss information in class.

3. **Get a note taker.** Have another student in your class make copies of his or her notes for you so that you can focus on the lecture and either lip-read, watch your interpreter, or reading from your captioner's computer. We are visual people, and every time we look down to write a note, we miss some new information. A note taker eliminates that risk by taking notes for you during the lecture. Many colleges will even pay note takers for their service.

4. **Get Power Points and other materials from the teacher.** This is a great way to make sure you don't fall behind in class and to review for tests and quizzes. Where our hearing peers can look at a PowerPoint slide and listen to the lecture at the same time, we unfortunately cannot. Our full attention is on the hands of our interpreter or the words popping up on the screen from our captioner. To make sure you didn't miss any information from the PowerPoint or other presented material in class, simply ask your professor or teacher to e-mail you the materials presented in class to review at home.

5. **Request seating.** Figure out what works best for your hearing-loss style. Be early to your first class with any given teacher and request whatever seat makes it easiest for you to hear the teacher to the best of your ability. For me, it was always a seat in the front row on the right of the classroom so that the teacher was on my left side and close enough in front of me for me to read his or her lips.

6. **Turn the captions on.** Teachers are typically required to only show videos with captions or give you a transcript of any video they show in class. All content must be accessible to every student in the classroom. Make sure to inform your teachers

that, if they are showing any videos in class, you will need them to turn on the captions. (Honestly, transcripts are not anywhere near as helpful as actual captions on the film. With transcripts, instead of looking up at the film, you are frantically looking up and down between the film and a piece of paper, trying to figure out what place the video is at.)

7. **Request priority registration.** Many colleges offer this option so that you can register for classes first and avoid professors with thick accents, heavy facial hair, or other features that may make it harder for you to succeed in their classes. All you have to do is ask.

8. **Educate before group projects start.** Let your groups for group projects know the best ways to communicate with you (in writing or through an interpreter, for example). Also let them know how you would prefer that they contact you based on your preferences (such as text and e-mail versus a conference call) when you are first assigned groups. This ensures you are kept in the loop when everyone is communicating.

9. **Know your rights.** Read the American's with Disabilities Act and know what you have the right to. Also, inquire within your school district or college to find out what services are offered locally to help you succeed.

I am not going to lie. Many teachers and professors will fight you on some of these accommodations and will not be kind or understanding. But your education is just as important as the education of your hearing peers, so do not ever give up on making sure you have just as much access to your education as they do.

Disclaimer

This book is a collection of stories from my life as I remember it. It is not perfect, and some stories are told out of chronological order for flow purposes. I do not represent the Deaf community. Nor do the Deaf community and I hold all of the same beliefs.

I am not giving medical advice, and the things that may have worked for me to overcome the obstacles in my life may not work for all others. I am not endorsing, nor am I discouraging anyone from, getting cochlear implants. I believe it is a personal choice to be made by an individual based on his or her lifestyle, personal needs, and beliefs after collecting all of the information on the procedure.

This book was written to tell my story from my point of view for its entertainment and inspirational value. I hope that you enjoyed it!